Totally Fulfilled

Totally Fulfilled

More Money, More Freedom, More Smiles, Less Stress

Dean Graziosi

Totally Fulfilled: More Money, More Freedom, More Smiles, Less Stress

Published by: Visionary Publishing

First edition

Printed in the United States

ISBN: 0-9773248-0-X
LCCN: 2005908572

Cover Design: Richard Aquan
Interior Design: The Printed Page

Contents

Dedication

I dedicate this book to my grandmother, Carmella Post. Your love, strength, encouragement, stability, and wisdom allowed me to be the man I am today. Your words will forever ring in my ears. As I write this book your health is failing fast, but your words are brighter than they have ever been. You were the first person to make me realize that anything was possible. Your unconditional love and support will last an eternity. I will love you always and forever. Thank you, Gram.

Acknowledgments

I'd like to thank my mother for overcoming huge hurdles and always putting her children first. Mom, your love and compassion, even in the midst of adversity, have changed the destiny of me and my sister Paula for life. You are our hero even though you don't believe it.

I am thankful that my dad taught me such a variety of things that have helped me diversify with confidence. I know he is in my corner unconditionally, and I am fortunate to have that.

I want to thank my sister, Paula, for always showing the strength it takes to overcome obstacles. Even though we live on opposite ends of the country, your loving support and caring, along with your wonderful family, warms my heart daily. I am so proud of you.

Melissa, thank you for being a special part of my life. You are the one person who witnessed my humble beginnings. Thanks for believing in me unconditionally. I am blessed to have you in my life, first as my wife, and now as a best friend.

I thank you, Jonelle, for being a shinning star in my life. You have been there for some of my toughest times and always had faith in me. You showed me a side of love I would have never known if I had not met you. Your loving support is empowering.

I thank my grandfather, Albert Post, who died when I was just ten years old. He showed me a love and caring that to this day still warms my heart. I think of you often and appreciate the time we had together, even though it was very short.

I want to thank all my friends who supported and loved me, even if they thought I was a bit crazy at some times. You were and are my family. Thank you for the laughs, the tears, and everything in between.

I also want to thank all the people who have come in and out of my life and who have helped me learn and experience such a variety of things. I feel blessed to have accomplished so much in such a short amount of time. I know nothing in life worth writing about can be done as just a sole venture. So I thank everyone who has taught me valuable lessons on what path to take as well as what path to avoid.

Part 1

The "Core" of Success

Introduction

This may not be a typical introduction; in fact, it will not be a typical book. I like to put myself in the shoes of other people, and if I were you, I would ask, "Who the heck is Dean Graziosi, and why should I read this book? What can he show me about living a more fulfilled life that's different from all the other advice out there?"

Here's my best shot at a short answer to that question: I know if you start to read this book, you will finish it. And if you finish it, I promise that your life will change forever. I don't think so, I *know* so.

Today, so many people go through their lives struggling to figure out how to be fulfilled or successful in just one area of life. To live a Totally Fulfilled life may seem impossible, but it's not.

Have you ever wondered why one person seems to have "it" while others struggle? Why do some people seem born under a "lucky star," and everything they touch turns to gold, while others, maybe even you, seem to work twice as hard but don't ever catch that lucky break?

Did you ever think that maybe the "it" that makes people happy and successful isn't luck? What if a guy who never went past high school, who read just a handful of books in his life, who came from a broken home, and who started with next to nothing, discovered simple strategies that could allow you to generate an abundance of wealth, happiness, peace, security, love, health and Total Fulfillment in every area of your life?

Well, I am that guy, and I am going to share that plan with you.

I'm not naïve or egotistical enough to tell you that I created what it takes to be Totally Fulfilled; successful people have always had these "core" tools at their disposal. But, through trial and error and my simple approach to life, I have found a way for you to make these core success principles a way of life for you, too. And once you have these secrets inside of you, you will realize that the only limits in your life are the ones you impose on yourself.

My parents divorced when I was three; we moved 20 times by the time I was 19. Each of my parents married and divorced three more times. We had very little money; in fact, my mom supported my sister and me by working two jobs to earn about $90 a week. In my blue-collar family, all my relatives and friends worked labor-intensive jobs for minimal pay. So my role models for true financial success were few and far between. Yet, starting with no money and only a high school education, I have been able to generate tens of millions of dollars, and I now probably make more money than 97% of the world.

So many people go through life with daily feelings of pain, scarcity, inferiority, stress, low self-esteem, frustration, lack of fulfillment, unhappiness, and so much else. Yet a small percentage of people seem to know something that others don't: How to live their life on another level. How to be grateful for what they have in abundance, not bitter about what they lack. How to change their beliefs to be limitless even in the face of adversity. How to focus on outcomes and solutions, not problems.

These people confidently hold their head up a little higher than most and are excited about the day ahead of them. They're calm when others are stressed and have an answer when others are frustrated. Other people look at this fulfilled group and long to have the same sense of peace with themselves and their surroundings.

Are these people lucky? Maybe a few are. But each of them shares a "core" for success that I will share with you in this book in an easy to digest and easy to apply format. I am going to say this a lot but will soon prove it to you: There is nothing in this world that someone else has or does that *you* can't have or do.

Now, you may be thinking, "How could this be possible in today's world? My life is already so hectic!" I will show you how by using simple techniques you can create a "core" inside of you that will allow you to succeed and be fulfilled in all areas of your life, at levels typically left for dreams. And it's easier than you could ever imagine!

Have you ever heard the saying: "To be successful, you have to be at the right place at the right time"? That's one of the greatest lies you and I were ever taught. A flat out lie! **In reality, you have to be the right person at the right place at the right time.** Consider this: If you give a below-average person a fantastic opportunity, he or she will struggle, just as in the past. On the other hand, if you give an above-average person even a mediocre opportunity, he or she will find a way to leverage that opportunity into something greater.

This statement is so powerful that I want to restate it as simply as possible: "An above-average person will always find a way to make it work." And an above-average person does not mean someone richer, smarter, or better looking, or someone who has had an easy obstacle-free life. By "above-average" I mean an exceptional person who follows a certain path. We all have an above-average person inside of us, and I want to show you how easy it is to bring that person out in the open.

Wouldn't you love not to be afraid anymore? To know how to overcome *any* obstacle in your way? To be able to embrace change and be thankful for its presence in your life? To bring all of the relationships in your life to a level that most people only dream of? To set goals that become reality, not just a dream sketched on a napkin?

We are going to explore the power of giving, letting go of the past, and focusing on where you want to go. How would you like knowing that, whenever problems arise, you can immediately focus on a beneficial solution and never ponder mistakes or problems again? This is just a fraction of what we will explore in this book.

If you're reading this book, you're excited about creating more wealth. You're excited about wealth in terms of money, happiness, and fulfillment. Or you could be looking for answers to change an unpleasant area of your life, and you are not sure how to do it. Either way, you're eager to achieve a life that is Totally Fulfilled.

Through my experiences, I have watched how people lacking in areas of their life get overwhelmed, feel that success or achievement in each area of their life is separate and apart from the others. The truth is, we can unify all areas of our life. Have you ever made ten different New Year's resolutions, then raced out and tried to accomplish them all at once, got overwhelmed, and ended up accomplishing none of them? This most likely happened because you saw each resolution as separate from the others, and each one seemed to demand a lot of sacrifice or work.

But if you can create a "core" approach to your life, you can easily accomplish and fulfill *all* aspects of it as if they were one. It's a strategy I wish *I* would have known about ten years ago, but *you* can know right now.

Allow me to pull you towards success. I can't make you successful if you are not ready to be, but I assume since you've read this far that we are a lot alike and you want to take action to change your life forever. Agree to be an active participant in the process of this book. Passive people typically get poor results, while action-oriented people get massive results. Results are what matter. You can produce whatever results you desire.

Money is a result. Happiness is a result. Fulfillment is a result. You can produce these results in your life.

Don't make the same mistakes I made. Ten years ago, if someone would have given me a book like this and said, "It will change your entire life forever," I know I never would have read it. I would have thought that my problems were personal and only I could figure them out. In retrospect, I was foolish. With a book like this, I could have started the journey towards Total Fulfillment much sooner, and would have been even further ahead today than I already am with a lot less stress and trial and error. Now that you have this book in your hands, follow me on this journey that will allow you to be in control of your life, your feelings, and your future.

I congratulate you for taking steps to create a life of wealth, abundance, happiness, accomplishments, confidence, love, prosperity, and so much more. So many people wait until their last years or even last days on this earth to realize what path they should have taken or how to learn from their mistakes. By then, they don't have the time or the ability to make those changes. But you have that chance right here, right now to start anew with an action plan for success.

Let's face it, we are going to live our lives, so shouldn't we get the most out of it? Ask yourself, "Do I deserve the best? Do I deserve success?" I have no doubt that the answer is "Yes." So then let's make it happen!

Chapter 1

Limitless Beliefs Equal a Limitless Life

"The greatest discovery of my generation
is that a human being can alter his life
by altering his attitude of mind."
—William James

I was a very late bloomer physically. In fact I didn't start to reach puberty until I was in high school. I weighed less than 100 pounds and stood well under five feet tall going in to the 10th grade. Worse, I had a high-pitched voice, so I got teased a lot. That wasn't too bad because I attended the same school from fifth to eighth grade, so people got to know me as a person, not just the small kid with the high pitched voice. But then the one thing happened that no middle school kid wants—I moved to another town and started at a new high school. Going to high school from middle school is hard enough, but combine that with being small, squeaky voiced, friendless, and until that point, being in a special reading class due to trouble in English all through middle school, and you can see my school life wasn't great.

Being small most of my life made me very shy, so making new friends was never easy. It didn't help that among a certain segment of kids I earned the nickname "Rocky." Not after the pugnacious boxer in the movies, but the squirrel from "The Rocky and Bullwinkle" cartoon. Girls thought I was cute but not dateable. Kids that would be friends with me during class would ignore me at lunch or recess. I could deal with that. But then the all time tragedy hit, swimming class in gym. After swimming class, everyone hit the showers and threw their suits in the basket, showered and got a towel. I was the only one in 10th grade whose head was the only place on their body with hair. You can imagine what happened with that ordeal. Let's just say that "hairless" and "squirrel" were tossed around.

Before I go further, I have to say that this is not a "poor me" story. I know there are so many people that have it much worse off than I did and I am sorry for that. I share this story and other events because they helped me become who I am today. I was able to use these challenges to propel me forward and not hold me back. I am hoping you will be able to relate to even one part of my experiences, and you can turn a past situation from an anchor to the wind in your sails.

...You can turn a past situation from an anchor to the wind in your sails.

Back to the story. My parents always told me, "You're a late bloomer. Don't worry about it." My mom, dad and my gram always tried to encourage me, telling me I was a great person. If people couldn't see that then it was their loss. They would tell me to be true to myself and in the end I would be the winner.

Absolutely amazing advice—except hard for a 10th grader to value—especially after the shower incident. But after 10th grade was over and I was still not growing, my father took me to the doctors. Good thing I went. For some reason, my body was not producing the right hormones to start puberty. So I was prescribed some sort of steroid and an appetite enhancer. I still remember Dr Kim and how he saved my high school life. Once I started the medication, I started puberty right away, I grew about 9 inches in a year and gained a bunch of weight. I am still only 5'8" but if I hadn't gone to the doctors I may have never grown any taller. So thank you Dr Kim.

Even before seeing Dr. Kim, I knew there was something inside of me growing; my outer appearance did not match what I was starting to feel on the inside. I didn't believe that just because I was smaller than other kids I was inferior in any way. I took the name-calling, the odd looks, and the negativity that was surrounding me and used it to my advantage. I'd say, "Someday I will show you all. No matter how big or small I am, I will succeed."

You know, a funny thing started happening—the more I told myself this, the more I believed it. I was growing both physically and mentally. By the end of 11th grade, I had a firewood cutting business and hired bunch of the bigger guys from high school to help split and carry the wood. These were some of the same guys who made fun of me just a few years earlier. I had an attractive girlfriend, I was making money, and I was starting to blossom as a person. Even though we had very little money while I was growing up, I bought a newer car that had been rolled over in an accident for next to nothing. I worked everyday after school with my father when I was fifteen to fix it up, and just a few months after I got my license, the car was done and it looked great. Thus, I was one of the few kids who had their own car. Best of all, I paid for it with minimal cash and sweat equity. It was a nice car and I was making money. I applied what I learned about hard work to school as well and by 10th grade I was in the regular English class.

I also started to believe that no one can make me feel inferior without my permission. I love the saying, "it's not the size of the dog in the fight, it's the size of the fight inside of the dog." Instead of being the victim, I turned the negativity into my reason for victory. I could have allowed my past to equal my future but instead I changed my belief and my destiny. I didn't need to change, but the way I saw myself needed to. In a way, Dr. Kim helped to guide me further along a path I was already heading down.

The Power of Perception

Our beliefs about ourselves, our perceived boundaries, and the people around us have a huge impact on where we think we can go in life. Beliefs allow one person to believe he or she can go to the moon, while another person may believe it's impossible to get even a $1.00 an hour raise.

We become the people we believe we are.

We get out of life what we *believe* we will get out of life. We become the people we *believe* we are. If you are successful in many areas of your life, your beliefs about yourself, your limits, and what you deserve are radically different from a person who thinks being successful in even *one* area of life is an overwhelming, even impossible task.

Remember, where you are in your life or where you have been in the past does not matter; you can always achieve more. Another level of success or fulfillment always awaits you around the corner. Do you creep up to that corner and peer nervously around it? Or do you stride confidently forward, eager to see what awaits you?

We all have limiting beliefs inside us whether we know it or not, and they may be the main reason some of us can't get to the next level in life. If you're not where you want to be, if there are parts of your life you wish you could change but just can't seem to, if you're not as successful as you should be, it's probably not your fault.

Chances are, without realizing it, you've been *conditioned for mediocrity*. Until now.

You've probably seen how a dog or another pet learns—through repetition or conditioning. Totally Fulfilled people follow a pattern for success, repeat that pattern over and over again, adjusting it as necessary, and condition themselves for success.

I'm sure you've heard the adage: "You are what you eat." The same principle applies to creating a Totally Fulfilled life. You are who and what you surround yourself with. Who do you listen to? Who do you hang around? What kinds of attitudes do those people and organizations have? They have helped to make you who you are.

You reflected the influences in your environment as you grew up and evolved through your adult life—your teachers, friends, parents, spouse, and others. From this programming, you developed your core personal beliefs—beliefs you may not be completely aware you have.

Core Attribute #1

Totally Fulfilled people are positive, optimistic people who create their own reality and don't let their past, other people's negative views of them, or life's challenges defeat them. They surround themselves with other positive people and condition themselves for success.

Think of beliefs in two different categories: those that may be holding you back and limiting your success in life, and those that have allowed you to excel, to take action, and to prosper. Before I give you specific techniques that will allow you to reach deep inside to find the beliefs that hinder you, *and* the ones that help you, take a moment and categorize a few of your beliefs to see which pieces of your past are drastically affecting your *current* life and your *future*.

You can go to *www.totallyfulfilled.com* and click on "FREE BOOK BONUSES" to print a Beliefs worksheet, or I have created one for you in the back of the book on page 282. On the left side of the page at the top, write "Limiting Beliefs." Beneath that, list all the things you can think of that seem to hold you back in life. On the right side, write "Limitless Beliefs," then list those qualities and beliefs that have allowed you to accomplish any of your goals to this point.

You may be reading this in a plane, in the passenger seat of a car, in your bed, or maybe even in the bathroom. That's okay. If you can't write anything down, simply take a few moments and really think about your beliefs.

Limiting Beliefs—They're What's Stopping You

"I've never been poor, only broke.
Being poor is a frame of mind.
Being broke is a temporary situation."
—Mike Todd

Okay, now that you've listed some beliefs on your own, let's go through some specific questions to narrow the focus of your beliefs even further.

Let's start with "limiting beliefs." As you think about this category, **answer these questions**. Write, or at least take a moment to think about a "yes" or "no" answer after each, as well as the first thing that pops in your head about each question. It's quite a list, I know. Pick and choose the questions that hit home. You will likely have more questions to pile on top once you get going.

◆ Do you believe making more money than you currently do is almost impossible? If you would like to make more money, how much would that be?

◆ Do you think your education and your intelligence level are major factors in determining how much money you can make?

◆ Do you think it takes money to make money?

◆ Do you believe that your relationship with a loved one or your family is as good as it gets, due to circumstances beyond your control?

◆ Do you believe failure or mistakes are a bad thing?

◆ Do you believe life handed you a raw deal or that you have had more obstacles than most people?

◆ Do you feel that family, friends, children, or even your boss are holding you back?

◆ Do you believe you have very little or nothing to be grateful for?

◆ Do you feel you have had very few accomplishments in your life?

◆ Do you think you have nothing to be proud of?

◆ Do you believe that change is scary? Do you fear the unknown?

◆ Do you wish problems would just go away forever?

◆ Do you take advice from people—a relative, a parent, or a spouse—just because they are older than you are?

◆ Are you bored with life, not knowing what excites you anymore?

◆ Do you feel that circumstances control the direction you are going?

◆ Do you feel frustrated, angry, upset, overwhelmed, insecure, fearful, guilty, or worried on a regular basis when you encounter unexpected problems?

◆ Do you ever say to yourself, "Why does this always happen to me?"

♦ Do you have a favorite belief or phrase that you use when things don't go your way like: "I could have made it if only _____ didn't happen"?

♦ Are you ever envious when other people get ahead? Even if you don't say it, do you feel it?

Like an outdated computer, we need to upgrade our beliefs and way of thinking.

No matter what your thoughts or answers are, your honesty is important here. The answers you provided do not make you any less capable of living a Totally Fulfilled life. Rather, we're identifying traits and beliefs that are holding you back. Consider the fact that by the time we're seven years old, we've heard the word "no" over 10,000 times!

So many of us have been programmed in all the areas of our life—money, relationships, business, health, success, etc.—and we don't even know it. Like an outdated computer, we need to upgrade our beliefs and our way of thinking. You are in control. It's time for you to purge your limiting beliefs and substitute them with more supportive, empowering, *limitless beliefs*.

Limitless Beliefs — Break Free From Your Past

"Courage is resistance to fear and mastery of fear,
NOT absence of fear."
—Mark Twain

Now let's go to the other end of the spectrum, the "limitless beliefs." As you think about this category, **answer these questions**. Again, answer a "yes" or "no" for each and write down any feelings associated with each one:

♦ Do you wake up each day knowing there are no limits to what you can do or what you can become?

◆ Do you feel the question is not "if" you can experience a fulfilled life, but "when"?

◆ Do you look at change as a challenge, not a fearful obstacle?

◆ Do you chalk up failures and mistakes as lessons and building blocks towards a better future and tomorrow's successes?

◆ Do you realize that the words or thoughts of others are merely their opinions, or their insecurities projected towards you?

◆ Have you realized that you can love your family, friends, and peers, but not have to agree with them or need their approval?

◆ Have you realized that you don't need anything in your life to succeed except you?

◆ Do you have the "juice" for life because you know there is more out there for you, and you are going after it?

◆ Do you appreciate everything you have accomplished in your life, whether big or small?

◆ Are you are thankful for the things you already have, whether big or small?

◆ Do you realize that problems and stress are part of life, and that you just need to know how to focus on the solution rather than on the problem?

◆ Do you believe in your heart that your past does not determine your future, no matter how difficult it may have been?

◆ Have you ever looked in the mirror and said, "I am proud of you"?

◆ Do you let other people know that you appreciate their opinions but that you are on a different course than they may be?

◆ Do you appreciate when other people do well for themselves?

◆ Do other people's successes give you even more motivation to go after your dreams?

◆ Do you say things to yourself like, "I deserve more, and I know I will find it"?

◆ Are you willing to learn from successful, fulfilled people? Are you able to learn from your own mistakes as well as the mistakes of others?

Take a moment right now and make sure to answer the questions honestly. Maybe add some of your current limitless beliefs in to the mix. Think of beliefs that are inside of you that have helped you to this point in life. **What belief made you pick up this book?**

In addition, right now, why not go back to your limiting beliefs—the ones you answered "yes" to in the first column—and let's transform them into limitless beliefs. We'll take the first step towards erasing those limiting beliefs inside of you that have held you back without you even knowing it.

> *Reframe your limiting belief into a limitless belief.*

Reframe your limiting belief into a limitless belief. For example, you can reframe the limiting belief "I believe my success and net worth are limited by my education and experience," as "My motivation and enthusiasm alone will attract opportunities for success like it has done for so many others."

Here's another example. Restate the limiting belief, "I believe it takes money to make money," as "I love knowing creativity and desire is what it takes to make money."

If you hold the limiting belief, "I have been dealt a bad hand in life," reframe it as "My past does not determine my future."

The limiting belief, "I have nothing to be grateful for," can be restated as "I am so fortunate to have _____ in my life, fortunate that my heart still beats every day, and fortunate that I get to re-invent myself as I choose."

Take a moment now to immediately give yourself the gift of limitless beliefs. I recommend transforming all or most of the limiting beliefs you have. See how easy it can be to change them and truly take in what that simple change can mean. Imagine how good it will feel when you can change your beliefs for life.

Take five or even ten of the limitless beliefs that touch you the most and read them aloud. If you can't do it now, then do it when you wake up tomorrow or before you go to bed tonight. As you say them, feel it. Feel that a Higher Power is listening to you. When you say them, please don't whisper or say them as if you're being forced to say them! Say them like you mean them! Let your subconscious know that things are changing!

A few years ago, this exercise helped me get through a very difficult time. This simple lesson saved my mental health and empowered me beyond belief. I have many businesses, and one was a small used car dealership I started for a friend. To make a long story short, the people who ran the dealership made some very poor decisions and got the company in debt quickly. Instead of coming to me when it first happened, they tried to fix the problem but only made things worse. Once I was made aware of the situation, I immediately had to come up with a significant amount of cash to pay off this debt.

At the same time that this was happening, I had several other situations with various companies that demanded a big influx of cash as well. Even worse, in some of the cases, people I cared about and trusted took advantage of me when I could have used their help. Of course, old, limiting beliefs started popping in my head, like, "Why do these things always happen to me?" and "How could people I trust do this?"

I found myself feeling overwhelmed, uncertain of the best road to take, and unsure whether I could even resolve the issues, so I took a walk to think. Practicing what I preach, I searched for my limitless beliefs. I reflected back on the past experiences that allowed me to come this far. Nothing I had done to this point had stopped my evolution towards a fulfilled, prosperous, and successful life.

I was thinking of other successful people I knew who had encountered worse situations than mine and came out stronger. All of a sudden, I started saying the phrase, "If I can get through this mess, I can get through anything." Each time I said it, the words came out with greater intensity and volume. In fact, at one point I literally had goose bumps all over my body. I shouted the words with passion: "If I can get through this mess, I can get through anything!"

I was commander of my ship, and no one could sink it without my permission!

This phrase empowered me, inspired me to take this lesson and move on, without letting anyone or anything knock me off track. I was commander of my ship, and no one could sink it without my permission!

Well, everything turned out fine, and I evolved to another level in life shortly after that. Plus, I took with me a whole new set of priceless, limitless beliefs and lessons for my future.

Why not memorize ten of *your* favorite limitless beliefs? When you need empowerment, you can say them out loud, feel them, believe them, and make them happen.

You are what you believe, and *you can do what you believe*. Who has the power to stop you? No one!

Chapter Check

- ❑ Reality is really what you perceive it to be.

- ❑ No one can have power over you unless you let them.

- ❑ Chances are, others conditioned you for mediocrity.

- ❑ Your path to success is only blocked by the Limiting Beliefs you and others have placed there.

- ❑ Your Limitless Beliefs allow you to access all the power of your "Core" to overcome those Limiting Road Blocks.

- ❑ To become Totally Fulfilled, transform your Limiting Beliefs into Limitless Beliefs.

- ❑ You are what you believe. You can do what you believe.

Now that we've taken a look at how Limitless Beliefs can help transform our lives, it's time discover the amazing power of attraction.

Chapter 2

Success Leaves Clues

"Whatever is impressed is expressed."
—Aristotle

About a year and a half ago I was working out at the gym. Being in my mid 30's, little aches and pains started that I chose to ignore. I was doing a shoulder press behind my back, and I felt something pop in my shoulder. It hurt terribly. As in the past, I figured it would just go away. But this was different, it just got worse and worse—to the point I could not lift my arm up to wash my hair. I could only sleep on one side, making for many sleepless nights. Finally I realized the injury was more serious.

I went to an orthopedic surgeon, got an MRI on my shoulder and they found that I had torn my rotator cuff. The doctor scheduled the operation to repair it. I just figured I didn't have an option and took his word as the only course of treatment. I surely could not leave it the way it was since I still experienced a ton of pain daily. When something is broken, you fix it. And when something is torn, you repair it through surgery.

I had a few months before the operation was scheduled since I put it off a bit due to work. Then by luck, I was having a conversation with a neighbor of mine. She told me I should do pre-hab—not re-hab—she called it pre-hab. I'd never heard it talked about that way, so I was intrigued. She suggested I go get physical therapy to strengthen the muscles around the tear. Her reasoning was that I should do so because after the operation, rehabilitation and recovery would be much faster. I took her advice, and I went to this simple little no frills rehabilitation clinic with just a bunch of great people working there. The owner asked why I was there and I explained.

...I live by the rule that there is nothing anyone else can do that I can't do.

He then asked me something I did not consider until that point. He said, "Did you ever consider not having the surgery and at least trying to do special exercises and specific shoulder strength training?" I asked him more about this new possibility, and he suggested a program where I started off very slow and worked up. I asked if it was possible to get my shoulder back to normal or even 95%, and he said many of his clients do. That was all I needed for the motivation to try it. As you know, I live by the rule that there is nothing anyone else can do that I can't do.

So, I started the exercise routine. At first my ego hurt, since I was barely using any weights, yet each week I saw improvement. I soon learned the routine, taking the information and doing those exercises at my own gym. Each week I gradually used heavier weights or did more repetitions without the pain getting worse. Then the pain started going away, and I started to get my shoulder strong again. I was washing my hair with no problems, I was able to lift my arm straight out to the side which I could not do before, and the best part was that I could sleep on my right side again. Of course, I canceled the operation and it has been over a year since the injury. As long as I don't go nuts and I keep my shoulder semi strong, it is 98% of what it once was.

This story illustrates how important it is to recognize when your beliefs are limited by a lack of knowledge. Also, I was limited by my perception that a doctor knew best and I shouldn't question his opinion. The man knew more than me, he was the expert so if he said have an operation, that was what I was going to do. Period.

But then the universe nudged me and told me that I should open myself up and be receptive to other ideas. I could have just as easily dismissed what I was told about physical therapy, but I didn't. By being open minded and willing to accept new ideas and being open to suggestions, I brought my neighbor to the point where she could make her suggestion. That's the power of attraction.

Core Attribute # 2

Totally fulfilled people are open minded and willing to consider that there are always multiple solutions to any problem.

Did you do the beliefs exercise (from p. 282)? I hope so. If you didn't, try to do it soon, because if you do it, you will be light years ahead of 95% of people in the world today.

Was the first group of questions—the limiting beliefs—or the second group—the limitless beliefs—easier for you to relate to?

Which ones were you able to whip through, with answers in your head as soon as you read them?

Which questions made you say, "I'll think about these, but they're not really 'me'"?

Would holding limitless beliefs be impossible with the life you currently have?

Did you think, "Dean, you're nuts! That's an impossible way to go through life"?

After you read this book, those limitless beliefs won't just be where you end up; rather, they will be the starting point of experiencing a *Totally Fulfilled* life. Changing your beliefs and realizing you have no limits is the first step. You can have happiness, wealth, and joy about life every day—something most people never get to experience.

If 100% of your "comfortable" answers fell into the second group—the limitless beliefs—then congratulations! You are among the top few percent of people in the world. By reading this book, you prove that you truly realize that being *Totally Fulfilled* is not about getting to a destination; it's an evolution. You probably also realize that what makes you feel successful or satisfied today may not make you feel that way in a year or even a month from now.

Putting the Pieces in Place

Just as healing a shoulder without surgery took sticking to an exercise routine, living a Totally Fulfilled life takes practice. And practice makes what?

Perfect.

"Practice makes permanent."

Wrong. This is another example of a limiting belief you've carried around way too long. The truth is "Practice makes permanent." If you practice something wrong over and over again, you'll do it wrong. If you practice something right over and over again, you'll do it right. Different way to look at it, isn't it? You and I weren't *taught* money, happiness, joy, prosperity or a Totally Fulfilled life. Therefore, we must be willing to let go of our false programming and allow a new program to replace it.

You want permanent change, not a temporary one. Wouldn't it be powerful to know that if you lost everything, you could get it back within a few months? People who live a Totally Fulfilled life know this to be true in all areas. I am not 100% certain that he is totally fulfilled in *all* areas of his life, but when it comes to his business accomplishments, Donald Trump is a good example. He lost everything, got it back within a few years, and now has blown past his prior beliefs. You can only imagine what his limitless beliefs are today.

I congratulate you for taking a step in the direction of change. Chances are, your belief system may be changing already. If you are like many people, and you found it easiest to relate to the limiting beliefs questions, *Change your beliefs, change your life.*

that's okay. Because you now possess one of the greatest secrets to changing the outcome of your life: *Change your beliefs, change your life.* Realize that we're just getting started. I promise you together we *will* change your beliefs and get you on the path of a Totally Fulfilled life.

Make Your Mind Ready for Greatness

> *"The world is what we think it is.*
> *If we can change our thoughts,*
> *we can change the world."*
> —H.M. Tomlinson

Let's go a little further and explore even more strategic steps you can take to start fresh with new beliefs—beliefs you can practice every day to stoke the fire within and provide the fuel to win the race called life.

As you've read, your false programming has been instilled in you in a variety of ways, including the influence of your parents and peers, and ideas about what each failure or success means to you. Your past programming sets the bar for your beliefs and your future. No matter what they are, if your beliefs don't support you, then you have to change them.

For example, I don't care if you are Republican or Democrat. I don't care what religion you are. In most cases, you are what you are because of your parents or other influences you had growing up. Did you research what religion you liked as a child? When you first registered to vote, did you research which party you liked? Maybe. But in most cases, you chose the belief system your parents or other people taught you.

So if your parents instilled beliefs in you such as, "Go to school and get a good job, because that is how you make it in life, and if you don't you may not have anything," then that could be an underlying limiting belief you have. Anything outside of that belief frightens you, and that belief may very well keep you in a job you dislike and at a level of income you hate. If your parents ran their own business at one point and failed, you may have inherited a limiting belief that makes you scared to death to try your own business, even though you have a strong desire to.

If you had friends or important people in your life who had wonderful, caring, nurturing relationships with their spouses, you may feel one way about relationships. However, if you had parents or influential people who had horrendous relationships, or felt they were abandoned, or if someone you looked up to told you that relationships are impossible and that you should stay single forever, then you may be afraid of commitment and not know why. Your beliefs are guiding you like a puppet on a string. So think hard once again and determine the limiting beliefs you have in all areas of your life.

Think of your experiences growing up that may still be affecting you today. As an adolescent, my limiting beliefs file was full. Luckily, I was able to chip away at each one month by month, year after year; I still find them and change them to this day. Having your mind filled with limitless beliefs and erasing limiting beliefs is not a one day practice. It's an ongoing gift you can present to yourself.

You can change your beliefs in an instant. You are what you focus on. You can truly have what anyone else has, once you believe you can. For example, when it comes to money, what if you thought like Oprah Winfrey, Paul Newman, Bill Gates, or Donald Trump? Donald Trump's mental money conditioning causes him to think like a billionaire—make that a multi-billionaire. Where would you be if you thought or had the mental conditioning he had?

Within a few years, a staggering amount of people who win over $1,000,000 in a lottery are back to the financial state they were in before they won. Yet someone like Donald Trump can lose it all and get it back. It comes back to his adjusted limitless beliefs and conditioning.

If you seized all the money from everybody in the world, and everyone had to start from zero once again, 95% percent of the money would end up back in the hands of the people who had it originally. At this point in my life, I know that is a reality.

By shifting your beliefs, you can live a Totally Fulfilled life. This is with all avenues of your life, not solely money. It's your time to unlock the door and utilize the power of focus.

Having More Money is Not Taboo

"I'd like to make footprints in the sands of time before I check out, but you can't make footprints in the sands of time if you're sitting on your butt unless your intent is to make buttprints in the sands of time."
—Bob Moawad

While we are on the topic of money, I want to share my thoughts about this "taboo" subject. Money is a tool in your toolbox that gives you more choices, allows you to enjoy greater happiness, and helps you get to the next level in your personal development.

I have had the opportunity to meet so many people, and having money is usually the first dream they have. Whether it *should* be a leading goal or not, let's face it, it is. I know I am good at not only creating money for myself, but also helping others to do the same. But keep in mind that we are building a core inside of you designed for success in every area of your life. Once that core is built, you can plug in anything you want to accomplish. If more money is one of your goals, it's going to happen.

Using the same strategies I am sharing with you in this book, I have been fortunate enough to have generated tens of millions of dollars in my life. I am living proof that there is no limit to how much money you can make, even if you have to start with next to nothing like I did. I understand, and you should too, that money alone will not lead to a fulfilled life, but it surely can help *expand* your life and reduce stress in many ways.

People don't want money for money's sake. They want money for the *feelings* they think it will give them. So imagining more money in your life is not selfish and it's not evil; it's okay.

If I hit a button, and instantly you had an extra million dollars in your bank account today, what are the top three things you would do with it? Maybe you would buy a new house for your family *for a feeling of accomplishment.* Maybe you would help out your extended family with financial matters *for the amazing feeling of giving.* Maybe you would help your parents or have your husband or wife quit a job they hate *for the feeling of sharing gratitude.* Maybe you would buy a hot new car and a new boat *for the exciting feeling of status.*

Money is not the root of all evil. Money alone, without your proper internal core, can go wasted and actually make you *un*fulfilled. Money does not buy you love, health, or happiness, but it can allow you to do amazing things for yourself and your family that spark enormous feelings inside you—feelings you will want to have over and over.

Used properly, money gives us the freedom to choose which door we walk through in life. It's your time to choose. Is a father of three who works sixty hours a week and who feels guilty about not spending enough time with his family greedy if he imagines more money in his life? What if just one thing in this book allows him to imagine and then realize that he already has it in him to overcome his personal obstacles and make a change? What if he challenges his limiting beliefs and starts to make more money in another way? Money would give him the *freedom of choice* and allow him more time to spend with his children.

What about the woman who would love to be a stay-at-home mom, yet her finances don't allow it? What if she could learn from this book that she has the tools inside of her to make a change with confidence? What if she is able to *choose* to overcome obstacles that may be in front of her and not only *imagine* a better life, but also have tools to *gain* it.

It's estimated that an overwhelming number of divorces stem from fighting over finances. Wouldn't extra money or more time give couples the opportunity to focus more on their relationship rather than on the stresses of bills and finances? Could money help save a marriage? In a case like this, the answer is absolutely.

What if you wanted to give to your family or to people in need? What if giving is something that makes you *feel amazing*? I believe each of us has a need and desire to contribute, and there's nothing like the power of giving. Could additional money allow this? Of course it could.

If you were able to make the money you imagined or work the hours you dream of, would you be able to exercise more often and eat healthier food? Maybe you could take more time off for yourself, de-stress, and improve your mental health. Could money be one of the tools to help in these cases? Absolutely!

I want you to realize that imagining you could make more money, dreaming of starting up your own business, embracing change by switching jobs, or working fewer hours to spend time with family are all excellent ideas! Soon we will talk about embracing change and specific techniques for you to make more money and make changes with confidence so you can be Totally Fulfilled.

Let yourself imagine what you really want, what will make you feel happy and totally fulfilled with no limits. If money is a big part of that dream, that's okay. Just break it down and learn what feelings you are looking for when you imagine attracting more money into your life.

The Foundation for Changing Your Beliefs

"Each player must accept the cards life deals him or her.
But once they are in hand,
he or she alone must decide how to play
the cards in order to win the game."
—Voltaire

I want to share my background with you and some of the beliefs I was taught while growing up. If you're thinking I was born like the people who can totally relate to the limitless beliefs questions on pages 16-18, you are mistaken.

Let me first say I love my parents very much and am fortunate to have them both in my life. However, they divorced when I was three and my sister and I lived with my mom in various places, from Gram's house, to trailers, to apartments. I moved about twenty times by the age of nineteen. My mom worked two jobs making a total of about $90 dollars a week to support my sister and me. My parents have been married three additional times each since then, and they are currently both single.

My mom felt very insecure, even though she was an amazing woman. These insecurities made her run—moving sometimes from one state to another—whenever problems became too much for her to deal with. My dad had a very troubled childhood, so he dealt with his pain through rage. He never physically abused us like his father abused him, but he was unaware of the guilt and heartache his actions caused my sister and me.

My parents' cars were so bad growing up that I made them drop me off down the block from school so the other kids would not make fun of me. I hated a lot of the clothes I had to wear because they were different from what most of the kids wore.

I know many people reading this have experienced much worse hardships than I have, but I want you to see the type of beliefs we can develop while growing up. I only told you a fraction of my experiences. But from what I revealed, can you imagine the beliefs I started to develop as a child? I carried with me a laundry list of negativity and limitation.

Take a moment to reflect back on your life. What are some experiences you remember hearing, seeing, or copying that influence your way of living? What beliefs did you observe or experience that have steered your life in a direction that isn't conducive to fulfillment?

If you have negative, limiting beliefs, take them and restate them as positive *limitless beliefs.* For example, despite what happened to me, I realize my parents did the best they could. I am the person I am today because of all of my experiences, and I love them for that. I choose to take the positive lessons from my parents and learn from them; just as important, I make completely opposite choices from those that they made in instances where I saw they did not get good results. Accept the challenge to recognize the past as an important part of helping you become the person you are today. It's time though, for you to move beyond it and become the person you are *destined* to be.

...become the person you are destined to be.

Who I became as an adult could have gone in any direction. Yet I have changed my destiny, my path, my beliefs, and the destiny of every generation that follows me. Wouldn't you love for that to be *your* legacy?

The Power of Attraction

I learned how to attract money, success, love, confidence and joy because I believed I could. And if I did it with little guidance, I have no doubt that as a team we can do the same for you. Today, I'm fortunate to help support my mom, dad, grandmother, loved ones, and friends financially and/or emotionally. It's an accomplishment that feels one hundred times better than I could have ever imagined.

Did I get where I am today because of my perfect upbringing, all the money my family had, or because I never hit any obstacles or hard times? NO! I discovered by accident that I'm in control of my own destiny, and the past does not determine my future.

Remember, being totally fulfilled is a journey rather than a destination. Today, at this very moment, I am totally fulfilled. However, I realize that if I stand still or don't continue my growth and learning, I may not be next week. Being totally fulfilled means you are always growing and evolving to another level.

You may have heard that "objects in motion tend to stay in motion." If you focus on the beliefs that nothing can stop you and you are moving every day—using the skills I will show you to pick up speed—then you will be in motion towards a new life. Yes, you'll have a few challenges along the way. If you let those challenges or negative beliefs get you off-track, then your momentum will be carried in the wrong direction. The less time you're off-track, the more time you're on. The success track is waiting for you.

The success track is waiting for you.

Chapter Check

❑ Totally Fulfilled people are open minded and welcome challenges to accepted ways of thinking and doing.

❑ When you open your mind, the universe responds with other solutions to your problems.

❑ Limiting Beliefs prevent most people from being open-minded.

❑ Practice doesn't make perfect, it makes Permanent.

❑ Money is not the root of all evil—know your reasons for wanting to attract it into your life.

❑ The past doesn't determine the future.

❑ Being Totally Fulfilled is a journey, not a destination.

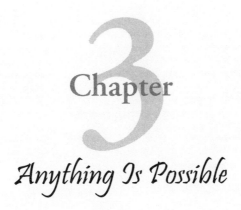

Chapter 3

Anything Is Possible

"You can't push anyone up the ladder unless he is willing to climb himself."
—Andrew Carnegie

Let me tell you a quick story about beliefs; it touches me more deeply with each passing year. One of my first mentors was my great grandfather. First, the word "mentor" is actually kind of a new term for me. I wish I had had a lot more mentors while growing up and even in my adult life. To me, a mentor is simply a person who has the answers to help you live the life you want and deserve. Their life lessons or their personal one-on-one touch can allow you to learn from mistakes and take advantage of the knowledge and accomplishments they have accumulated. They help you realize your dreams, eliminate your fears so you can see the light at the end of the tunnel, and help you pass through the tunnel to find another tunnel to conquer.

Mentors can be a variety of people, including family, friends, your boss, loved ones, and even a coach. Tiger Woods still works with a coach, right?

One of my first mentors (someone I've never even met) was my great-grandfather. He indirectly inspired me to raise the bar on my beliefs and helped me appreciate what I have. His story, told to me by my grandmother, allows me to appreciate the smallest things. How is this possible, especially since I never met the man?

Well, my great-grandfather's story begins at the turn of the 20th century, when he left a tiny town in Italy called Potenza with a belief that he could get more out of his life and give more to future generations. So my great-grandfather left Potenza and made it to the closest port that had ships going to America.

> *...what he didn't have in money he made up for with a strong desire and creativity.*

He wanted the chance for a better life; however, he had less than $5 in his pocket. But what he didn't have in money he made up for with a strong *desire* and *creativity*. He knew one thing for certain: he wanted to get on the ship. So he made a deal to work on the ship in exchange for a free ride to America.

Instead of limiting his beliefs and looking at all the obstacles, he focused on what he wanted. When the ship docked in New York City, he was dumped at Ellis Island. He couldn't speak English. He didn't know anyone. He came here alone. He left his family and all his comfort zones behind.

What was his belief? He believed there was a better life in America, and he went for it. Let's fast-forward a few years. He married my great-grandmother and moved to the little town I grew up in. They had four children, and he ended up owning his own restaurant.

When he arrived in America, he worked as a dishwasher but believed he could do more, so he worked his way up to being a waiter. Again, he believed he could do more. Eventually he saved enough money and found the courage to leave the city and move to a little town called Milton, New York where he opened his own restaurant.

He didn't stop there. He continued to save even more money. Why? Because even though he was making money, he believed his children were Americans and he wanted them all to go to college. I never got to meet him, but I did get to meet one of his four children—my grandmother, who is one of the dearest people in my entire life. From her, I learned a lot of great life lessons. Whatever problems I had growing up, they can't compare to what she had to overcome.

When she was twelve, my grandmother's mother died in her arms. My grandmother had to quit school and to take care of her younger siblings. As if that weren't bad enough, a few years later, when my grandmother was fifteen, my great-grandfather, who was also a part of his local fire department, was killed when the town's fire truck overturned.

Now here was my grandmother, who at age fifteen had lost both her parents and had four younger siblings to care for. Fortunately, my great-grandfather had saved enough money for her to live on and raise the other children. My grandmother took control and ran the household by herself. Even though she was just fifteen and only had a seventh grade education, my grandmother was able to budget the money and raise all the children until the youngest turned eighteen. She never once thought of the negatives. She didn't focus on the awful situation; she focused on something more important to her—her brothers and sisters, and her father's faith in her to manage the money for them to live.

Can you see why my grandmother is my greatest mentor, my inspiration, and so much more? I thank God I was able to know her so deeply and learn so much from her before Alzheimer's disease took much of her mind.

Even though my parents were divorced, and we had no money and a million other obstacles, I still had 100 times more than my great-grandfather and my grandmother had.

Even today, as I write the story, it inspires me on a new level. Oftentimes, the acres of diamonds we're looking for are right in our own backyard. The guidance or motivation we need could be right in front of us.

Core Attribute #3

Totally Fulfilled people are passionate and committed. Like my great grandfather and grandmother, they have passionate dreams of a better life for themselves and others. They are willing to do whatever it takes to make sure that others are cared for. They don't view this as a sacrifice but an honor.

Do An Honest Assessment

I hope by now you've begun to reach deep inside yourself and be honest enough to see how your beliefs are created and the impact they have on your life. Now that you have come this far, let's say this again: "Your past does not determine your future." Write that on your forehead if you have to. What your peers think, what your family taught you, what you think people expect from you, what you did yesterday or last year or in the last ten years has nothing to do with what you could start doing today and tomorrow.

When you talk about wanting more out of life, do people tell you to be happy with what you have? That life isn't perfect? Well, if you really felt that was the truth, then you wouldn't be reading this book. What those people are saying is nonsense; don't believe it. Ask yourself, "Are they qualified to give me advice? Do *they* live a totally fulfilled life? Do they make the money they would really like to make and have a job they love? Are they in a perfect relationship? Do they smile more than frown?"

Make a mentor out of someone who has the results you want...

Be careful who you take advice from. Make a mentor out of someone who has the results you want; then do what they do, and you could get what they have. If those offering advice don't have the results you want, why listen to them?

For many years my father and I had a roller coaster relationship, which I'm sure many of you can relate to. One moment, he would be the wind in my sails, then in an instant, things would change. His limiting beliefs kicked in, and he projected them on to me.

He thought I was crazy each time I did something outside his belief zone. When I got a new house, he said, "The house is too big. You're going to lose it." When I started a new business, he said, "That's crazy. You're stepping outside of what you know." He used to tell me, "You're too nice to people. You're going to get taken advantage of."

I know he said these things only because he loved me, and his limiting beliefs were telling him to think that way. These limiting beliefs could have been mine and almost were.

I am fortunate that today my dad and I have a great relationship and now he has completely changed from those days. I think if I called my dad tomorrow and said I was going to Mars in a month, he would ask me to bring him back some red rocks!

I did not allow my dad's beliefs, my past experiences, my failures, or other people's input to determine my beliefs and my future. Whether it was my grandmother's influence or I just was lucky to be born with it, I was creating limitless beliefs for myself daily. Now you can give that gift to yourself.

You have to get control of your beliefs first. Your beliefs won't and don't change after you get a promotion, or once you finally start your own business, or after the kids go to college, or after you retire. Your beliefs will not change on their own and they will hold you back if you don't change them right now. So let's do it!

It's easier than you think. You have to trust me and work at it. Will it take some practice and persistence? Yes. Is it worth it to wake up excited every morning because you're Totally Fulfilled as the captain of your ship, getting closer and closer to living your dreams? Absolutely!

Chapter Check

❑ Totally fulfilled people are generous—not always financially but with their time, experience, and talents.

❑ Your beliefs won't change on their own.

❑ You must take control of your beliefs.

❑ Generously give yourself the gift of limitless beliefs.

Chapter 4

It's a Bright New Day

"Circumstances do not make the man or woman,
they merely reveal them."
—Brian Tracy

To date, I have shipped hundreds of thousands of programs to people to help them make money with cars and Real Estate. So even if a tiny fraction of people are not happy, it still could be a few thousand people and the unhappy people usually voice the loudest opinions. To top it off, there are "Strategic Marketers", whom I would rather call "Unethical Marketers", that use my exposure on TV to create so called "Review sites" on the internet—they trash me or my program, create fake testimonials and then at the bottom of their page they say—but if you want the best home based business available today buy mine!!

When I first saw these things pop up it, it was very disturbing. I was being portrayed differently than who I was. Pretty

...a success mentality teaches you not to waste energy on things that you can't change.

upsetting. But experience, my own advice and a success mentality teaches you not to waste energy on things that you can't change. At least not at that very moment. I also know that no company is perfect and mistakes are made but my Customer Service Department does all they can to create total satisfaction. But sometimes no matter what you do you can't satisfy everyone. I want to share with you a recent email exchange that I had with someone who purchased one of my Real Estate courses. He somehow got my personal email address. I only share this with you to show my own evolution. Five years ago I would not have handled this situation in the manner I do today.

This man had sent several emails to the customer service department. They tried to help this individual but he was not satisfied. Shortly after these email exchanges, I got my first email with the subject line: **Wrong Victim**

Here is the exact text of what he sent:

You guys just made a big mistake. You have no intention of returning my refund requested money. I am right now happily sending a letter to the Attorney General of Arizona and West Virginia. I am requesting a full investigation of your money return practices. I stupidly fell for your infomercial (which now I taped for evidence in court) and I sent my hard earned money to a bunch of thieves (which soon will be investigated) for the amount of $110.10 on 22 August 2005 for some worthless brochure and DVD's. I returned the worthless merchandise back and I still haven not received my refund money. It looks that you guys have no intention of returning my money as advertised, so guess what!!! I am sending a letter not only to the Attorney General of Arizona and West Virginia but I will send this issue to the FBI, Internet Fraud Division, CNN, CBS, FOX, I already contacted some of them and they are very interested on my case.

Also due to the mailing of the brochures back, to the Post Master General, and Consumer Advocacy Agency and many many other, even the newspaper in Phoenix Arizona, So, you pick the wrong victim for your scam. I already sent my complaint to the Attorney General's. I am also setting a web site to collect story of individuals you had scammed for a class action lawsuit.

You just picked the wrong victim.

You have until Friday December 2, 2005 to return my money or else I will go beyond the Attorney Generals.

Also, I bought down a company in California for failing to return a manufacturers rebate to me — _____Co. I got them down very good. My lawyers smell money on your scam and practices. So, you either return my money or else.

I talked to _____ and _____several times and they always say the check is in the mail. No more games. Let's fight in court and see who wins?

A few years ago I may have reacted differently but I took a deep breath and looked at what he may have been feeling. Here's my reply:

Dear XXXX

I am sorry to hear what you have gone through. I just made a phone call and sent out two emails so I can get to the bottom of this. Customer Satisfaction is a very important thing to me and I am disappointed in your bad experience. I will make sure this is resolved ASAP and find out what happened.

Thousands of people each month get set up with the program and most everyone is happy and if they are not they get a refund right away. But unfortunately human error makes for a minimal amount of mistakes and a minimal amount of people slip through the cracks. It looks like you may be one of them..

Either way since you brought this to my attention I am all over it!!!

Quick question—What program did you get that you did not like? I am curious.

Sincerely,

Dean Graziosi

Shortly after that, I received this reply:

Hi Dean:

Thanks for your help and concern. I would like to tell you what happened but my lawyer told me not to talk to you guys about this issue anymore without his permission. He will not be back from vacation until next week.

Thanks for your assistance in this matter.

I was disappointed to hear that he was relying on his lawyers and not on the possibility that this could have been an easily resolved mistake. (Remember that Totally Fulfilled people are open-minded and are willing to look for alternative solutions and give others the reasonable benefit of the doubt.) Here's my next response to him via email:

Dear XXXX

I am sure this will work out.

I know how frustrating things like this can get—but try not to waste anymore energy on this because it will be resolved. Focus on more exciting things. And if you are an entrepreneur, as it seems you may be, find a passion whether it is Real Estate or something else and don't let anything stop you from taking your life and your finances to another level. I mean that from the bottom of my heart!!!!!

You are obviously a follow through type of person—use that energy and never give up and following through with your dreams

Take care and Happy Holidays!!

His final response to me after he talked to the Customer Service department and his bank:

I am very sorry for jumping the hoop so fast on you guys. You were right the bank had my money all this time. Their rep gave me wrong information. Thanks to the credit refund receipt faxed to me by you, they "mysteriously" found the money on my account but "not deposited"!?

Hmmm?

They are sending the money to me now and I told their supervisor Linda, to send an apology to you guys. She will be faxing and apology to the fax number used by _____, to your attention.

I am very sorry and I will make sure I update this incident in the www.xxxxx.com web site.

I will also contact the Attorney General of Arizona and West Virginia and tell them about the correction made.

If there is anything else you expect from me let me know.

Case closed. In the old days, I could have escalated my tone to match his and gotten into a confrontation with him. But I've learned over time that it's not worth it. I can choose where and how to spend my energy, and the couple of minutes it took to write a pleasant email and start the investigation into the matter was far less than if I had really taken his nasty tone to heart and then stewed about it all day. I chose to release that negative energy

I can choose where and how to spend my energy…

and turn it into something positive. I think or at least hope that I made some sort of difference in his life and maybe he will be more open and use his energy more wisely in the future.

Choose Your Day

Remember, you are what you focus on.

Remember, you are what you focus on. Each and every one of us does one thing every day—we wake up. How we wake up can kick off the entire day. Do you currently wake up looking forward to a new day, or do you wake up just prepared for another non-eventful daily routine? Do you hit the snooze button three times wishing it would all go away? Do you wake up in fear and stressed about the day to come? These are just a few of many ways that you could start your day.

It's your choice.

Any other way than waking up looking forward to a new day—a day filled with accomplishments—is limiting you and your life.

That may sound tough to do, and again you may be saying, "Yes, but you don't know what I have to deal with," and you are correct. But I have been fortunate enough to meet people who overcame obstacles one hundred times greater than I could have ever imagined a person could handle. Even these people can start their day with vibrancy and handle anything that comes up without taking a step backward. How? Because they have the "core" aspects inside of them for success so they succeed in all areas of life no matter what the obstacles. And we are starting to build that core in you right now.

The next secret I am going to share with you took time to develop. Yet once I did, it immediately changed my life forever. In my business, my finances, and my life, I am willing to make sacrifices and take chances; I take action to get what I want. And, like many people—maybe even you—I had no one to fall back on. If my ventures didn't work, or I lost everything, I did not have anyone I could go to for financial help.

I believed I had totally overcome any limiting beliefs that kept me from having faith in myself and going for the things I wanted. But I learned otherwise. While it didn't hold me back from going after what I wanted, for years I'd wake up sick to my stomach, nervous, anxious, and stressed. I still was getting ahead and accomplishing many things, yet I didn't feel good inside. Part of me was still fearful.

Finally, I cracked the code and figured it out: My limiting beliefs were still in control. I never gave myself credit for all I had accomplished, and for all the amazing people who were in my life. I forgot about where I came from. I forgot I had surpassed the goals

> *I never gave myself credit for all I had accomplished...*

I had once set for myself a thousand times over. I forgot I had been dealt many bad hands in my life, that I had hundreds of failures, and that I was broke many times, yet I got through it all.

Gratitude Transforms

And then I looked around at the people who were most successful and realized they had gotten through very tough times as well and came out stronger, smarter, and more fulfilled. It all boiled down to this: I was not grateful for all I had, for all I had done, and for all the amazing people I had in my life. I wasn't thanking God enough for giving me the skills to be the man I am. I forgot to be thankful that I was healthy and so was most of my family.

Once I realized this, I became grateful, and the more I appreciated what I had or had done, rather than what I didn't have or failed at, the knot in my stomach started to go away.

No matter what is going on in your life, no matter how difficult your past or how heavy the stress on your shoulders, you can wake each day excited about life, grateful for what you have (and hope to have), and ready to accomplish new things.

Core Attribute #4

Totally fulfilled people are Grateful. They choose to focus on what they have and not what they lack. They understand that many people contribute to the successes they enjoy— family, friends, colleagues—and they express their gratitude often and openly.

Start Your Transformation Now

You could truly wake up tomorrow feeling better than you have possibly ever felt in your life, and if you make it a part of your morning, the feeling can last forever.

Take a second and visualize yourself waking up tomorrow. Imagine yourself waking up with *a new, vibrant attitude*, no matter what happened the day before. In fact, you got up ten minutes before the alarm went off because you didn't want to waste any time starting your day. You have a new day to experience, and you can't wait to *make the changes in your life and beliefs.* You take a deep breath, and you are *grateful for another day* ahead of you.

...experience everything as if it were your last day

For the first time you can remember, it feels like the first day of a new life, and you want to *experience everything as if it were your last day* here on earth.

You look in the mirror, and you see that your outside appearance resembles the new inside of you. Your shoulders are back, your eyes are wide open, and you have a smile that's *brimming with confidence*. You're not only ready for what life hands you, but also for the things you want to change. You're *ready to accomplish new things* today rather than just handle the things you are concerned with, and the difference between the two is perfectly clear. As you walk out the door to start your day, you have a skip in your step because you know unequivocally that *you are in control of your future.*

Did you really try to picture it? Did you let you mind and body feel how amazing it would be to experience that every morning? If you can imagine it, you can do it.

Shed Limiting Beliefs for Good — And Live Each Day to Its Fullest

> *"You don't have to get it perfect,*
> *you just have to get it going."*
> —Mark Victor Hansen

I hope you let yourself actually feel a great morning. Let's get to how you can do that *every day* in less than ten minutes. Then we will go right into making each day even more amazing, and we'll cover special tools and safety nets so nothing can trip you up.

If what I am about to ask of you seems a bit odd, please trust me and try it anyway for just one full week. I promise your life will change forever if you do.

Tomorrow, wake up, and as soon as your eyes open, jump out of bed as if you were going to pick up your million dollars in Lotto winnings. Take a look in the mirror, and no matter what stress you had from the previous day, I want you to erase it from your exterior body. Put your shoulders back, open your eyes wide, and take a deep breath. The inside and the outside have to match. Even if you are faking it the first day, within a few days it will be real.

Before you think about anything for the day—your work, your boss, the bills, your relationship, or the things you *don't* have—take a few minutes and search deeply to uncover what you have to be grateful for: your health, a roof over your head, the heart in your chest. Whatever it is, find it and be thankful.

Take a minute and give thanks for the special people currently in your life and for those who may have touched you along the way, such as your parents, grandparents, special friends or relatives, husband or wife, your children, and any others. Think of the amazing lessons you have learned from them. Thank God or your Higher Power for allowing you life and the ability to control your own destiny.

Be proud of yourself for a moment, and reflect on the accomplishments you may have forgotten you achieved. We all have accomplished so many things, but when we are down we forget them. Maybe you can think of your first job, winning at a sport, your wedding day, the birth of a child, helping someone in need, being creative when others were not, being the best parent you can be, or making sacrifices so others could have more. Reach inside, find your accomplishments, and remember them with a smile on your face. Be proud of yourself, if just for a moment and let it feel good. You deserve it.

Take a moment and wish good things for those who may need it and have even tougher obstacles than you do. It's always good to remember others.

Now, think of the things you would love to accomplish, rather than thinking of the problems of yesterday or the problems that *could* happen but haven't yet. Realize we will always have problems. They will never go away, until the day we die. How we *handle* problems is what either creates or removes stress. The bigger and better your life gets, the bigger your problems get. After you read this book, however, you will be able to handle any problem in a fraction of the time *and* eliminate the fear, stress, anxiety and many other feelings that once accompanied problems.

As you start your day, visualize what your perfect day would be like:

- How would you start today if you truly believed anything is possible?

- What would you do at work?

- Would you start working on that special project?

◆ Would you start making notes of your dream job or dream business?

◆ Would you talk to someone you have been too shy to approach?

◆ Would you work on your current relationship to make it better than ever and more passionate?

◆ Would you tell someone you loved them?

◆ Would you start taking better care of your body and health?

Without limiting beliefs, you will not only dream about these accomplishments, but you can also make them happen. So picture the day as if everything you dream about is going to happen. The key is to begin with the end in mind.

I know it sounds like a lot to do at the start of your day, but it actually takes only a few minutes. I'll even make it super simple for you: Go to *www.totallyfulfilled.com* and click on FREE BONUSES, or go to page 290 and use your daily tracking sheet for the previous exercise!

If you make it part of your routine to practice these simple lessons, your life will start to change in all the ways you want it to.

Throughout the day, give yourself more credit than you may usually do. Most people are great at finding fault in themselves— we've been trained to look at what's wrong instead of what's right—but now see your strengths and take advantage of them.

Find your supposed weaknesses and see if they exist because of your beliefs. Then use the methods in this book to realize that your weakness may actually be your greatest strengths. It may be something you can change in an instant once your beliefs change.

Take this process a step further by writing down the things you have done well or accomplished without even realizing it. Force yourself to come up with several answers. Again, the worksheet I provided at

Truly know that no one human being is better than another...

my web site or the back of this book will have all these questions outlined so you can simply plug in your answers.

Have faith and the confidence to know you can quickly overcome any obstacles that come your way. Truly know that no one human being is better than another—no matter their upbringing, how much money they have, their education, or what part of town or the world they grew up in.

Instantly recognize a "Dream Stealer" (more on these people later, but the name says it all) and let their words bounce off of you. Remember that even the words of family, friends, supervisors, or co-workers can't limit your beliefs. It is much easier for people to bring you down to their level rather than to try to raise themselves up to yours. Don't hate them; rather, feel bad that they do not know what you know.

You have to pull the weeds and nourish the seeds.

On the other hand, surround yourself with people who support your vision and dreams and who will encourage you throughout the day. Model your own life after people with successful and fulfilled lives and take their advice.

You're planting seeds for a life Totally Fulfilled. You have to pull the weeds and nourish the seeds. It takes no effort at all to grow weeds in a garden. Anyone can grow weeds. Plant your seeds of limitless beliefs, water them, give them sunlight, pull those weeds, and soon you'll have a full ripe Totally Fulfilled apple tree giving fruit to everyone you meet.

I have given you a simple daily system that takes just minutes each day. When you see how little effort it takes to create your Totally Fulfilled life—mentally, physically, socially, spiritually, and financially—using this system for just a few days, you'll want to use it for the rest of your life.

Remember, you can print out a cheat sheet of a daily routine for success at our web site or you can use the one on page 290. Put one at home, one at work, and one in your car. It's worth it to be reminded you deserve more.

Think about it. If you wanted to learn how to speak Spanish, you wouldn't go to one class and expect to speak fluent Spanish for the rest of your life. You need to adopt daily patterns so your old beliefs don't pop back in and stop you dead in your tracks. If you want to change, you can. All it takes is practice. In just a few minutes each day, you can follow my daily action plan and not let your old beliefs hold you back from limitless new goals and dreams.

Finally, when something comes up and you have to react, or if you are thinking of making a change or taking a step in a new direction, you may feel fearful, scared, or unsure. If this happens, repeat the simple routine below.

So when something happens ask yourself these four questions right away:

◆ Is this (whatever the event or circumstance is) going to kill me?

◆ Am I going to go totally broke and not be able to feed myself or my family?

◆ Am I going to hurt anyone with the action I take?

◆ If I don't try this, or do something different, will anything change?

If you answer "no" to these questions, then go on to the next four quick questions:

◆ Can taking this step improve my life?

◆ Have I or anyone I know ever been in a similar circumstance and got through it OK or even better off?

◆ Am I scared because I feel I can't accomplish this, or are old limiting beliefs holding me back?

◆ Is this step or action what a successful or Totally Fulfilled person would do?

If you answer "yes" to any one of these questions, then you know your answer is to brush off the old you, the old limiting beliefs holding you back, and *go for it*.

This simple daily routine, along with everything else you have learned in this section, are the secrets to change the limiting beliefs that society and your peers have instilled in you.

Limited beliefs equal a limited life. Your past does not determine your future, and there is nothing anyone else has done that you can't do.

Part One of this book is designed so you can truly visualize patterns that will allow you to open yourself up for success. Now you can fill your thoughts, your mind, and your body with the ability to achieve anything in life you desire. With the right core and the right foundation, you can build anything you want on top of it.

Now, let's pick up the pace and eliminate anything that may get in the way of your total success and fulfillment.

Chapter Check

❏ You choose how to respond to other people and the attitude you will have.

❏ Gratitude can transform your outlook and your life.

❏ Daily practice of expressing gratitude for all you have will make a permanent change.

❏ You don't have to get it perfect right away, you just have to keep practicing it.

❏ Change takes time and persistence.

❏ Your past doesn't not determine your future.

❏ By transforming Limiting Beliefs to Limitless Beliefs, you tap your potential to achieve anything you desire.

Section Summary

❑ Reality is shaped by your perceptions.

❑ You have control over how you respond to others, your environment, and your past.

❑ You can shape your future and attain whatever you desire.

❑ Transforming your Limiting Beliefs to Limitless Beliefs will give you a limitless future.

❑ When you open your mind to all possibilities, the universe will offer you a solution to your problem.

❑ The road to becoming Totally Fulfilled is a journey and not a destination.

❑ Following a working model and through practice you can change your reality.

Core Attributes of Totally Fulfilled Individuals:

◆ Positive / Optimist

◆ Open Minded

◆ Passionate

◆ Grateful

Part 2

Chapter 5

Imagine the Possibilities with No Obstacles

"Ideas are the root of creation."
—Ernest Dimnet

I'm confident that the previous section opened your eyes and mind to beliefs that may have been inside of you—maybe even deep inside you—that have been holding you back and limiting your life. I hope you now see that we truly have no limits, just the ones we place upon ourselves or the ones we think others may be placing upon us. Once we eliminate those, a whole new path of life starts to open.

Take the time to continue this journey with me towards a life of abundance beyond what most people can even imagine. You're worth it!

The Power of Visualization

I know it may seem a bit odd, but do this with me: Remember when you were a child how great it felt to imagine and pretend? In some cases you could lose yourself in the moment and imagination would become reality. If you never did that as a child, try it for the first time with me now.

Picture yourself two years from today. Imagine your ideal life complete with all your new experiences. Take just a minute and write a brief description of what your ideal life would be like. I know you may face obstacles, and we will overcome them soon. But for right now, pretend you have no limits, no boundaries, and no obstacles. What would your ideal life look and feel like?

- How much cash would you have every week and how would you spend it?

- Who would you be with?

- What would your body look like?

- Would you smile more?

- What stress would be gone from your life? What happiness would fill the space stress left?

- Who do you see yourself waking up to every day?

- What is your health like?

- Do you have children? How much time do you spend with them?

- What would your relationship with God be like?

- How confident would you be? How would you express it?

- What type of people would you socialize with?

- Would you own your own business?

- Would you finally try to invent that idea you have had for years?

◆ Would you be retired?

◆ Would you travel?

◆ Would you have a college fund for your children?

Stay with me here, because this is only the beginning. Don't think I am going to leave you here with a page full of empty dreams. I am going to give you the keys to make them real *and* expand your current dreams to a much higher level.

So, let's go one step further. I want you to picture yourself with just one of your major goals, the one that would have the most positive impact on your life. Maybe the one that sparked you to get my book?

For example, let's say you want a dream house for you and your family. Picture yourself walking up to the front door of your dream house. What do you see? What is the landscaping like? See yourself entering the front door. Now look to your right and to your left. What do you see? Picture it as vividly as you can. What do you smell? Is there an aroma of flowers or cookies? What do you hear? Are children greeting you as you come in? Or pets? Or your spouse?

As you walk into the living room, what's it like? What do you see there? What do you see outside? Really try to picture it. Try to feel it and even write it down if you can. Where is the sun? Is there a lake, ocean, golf course, mountains, trees, backyard, swimming pool, or playground within your view?

Take in the moment and truly visualize being in your dream house and all the things associated with that, and then notice how you feel inside. Do you feel accomplished, confident, secure, or maybe just happy? Describe your feelings in writing if you can or take a few moments to really feel them.

Give yourself permission to dream. In your imagination, as you walk by a mirror, what do you look like? Has your weight changed? How are you dressed? How does your heart feel? Do you have a smile on your face?

I used the example of visualizing a dream house because so many people long for that sense of security a home gives, but you can do this with any and all of your major goals or wishes.

If you truly allowed yourself to imagine and dream for even a moment that it really was as you pictured, then congratulations! If you couldn't picture it yet, don't worry. In their early teens, most people forgot how to imagine. You simply need to remember what it was like being a kid. Remember the childlike enthusiasm and innocence you had when you thought about what you wanted to do

Success requires imagination...

that hour or that day, or what you would be someday. It was easier then, as a child, before life may have made you believe otherwise.

Success requires imagination, so doing this exercise is one of the most valuable skills to building a core inside yourself that can make anything possible. Believe me when I say your dreams are only an inch away from reality.

An Epidemic of Dissatisfaction

Just being an adult can sometimes rob us of our dreams, can't it? The overwhelming majority of Americans are going to retire broke, and most spend their lives in jobs they hate. Can we attribute this to a failure of our imagination? According to *www.mediate.com*, "The divorce rate in the United States is the highest in the world, with 50% of marriages ending in divorce." According to the Surgeon General's web site, "61% of Americans are overweight or obese," and the Center for Disease Control says, "By 2020, depression is expected to be the second leading cause of worldwide disability and the number one disabling condition in the developing world."

So many people are feeling so much pain and disillusionment that they can't imagine changing the direction their lives are going. That doesn't have to be the case. Everyone can alter their belief system; everyone can imagine and dream and then put a plan in effect to accomplish it, no matter what the obstacles are.

From Imagination to Reality

Here is an example of dreams becoming reality in the business world. When Federal Express first started, I remember everyone going crazy that a package could be delivered anywhere in America—and later the world—overnight. That notion transformed everything. Then, over time, we got used to it, and the service was no big deal. I remember when I got my first fax machine and could transmit a document to someone instantly. It seemed impossible that a phone line could carry a written message. Then, after a while, we got used to it. Then the Internet and e-mail hit, and now you could access almost any information and share pictures and documents with people around the world. Impossible! But now it's our way of life, and we are used to it.

Well, for each of those innovations, someone had to imagine them first. All of those devices and services started as a thought in someone's mind. They then made those ideas concrete and shared them with the world. While the results may be different, when you visualize something you want for yourself and your family, you'll be following the same steps to create a new reality. If our reality is a product of our thinking, why do we not think better thoughts to improve our condition? As you know from reading Part One, the answer is simple: we let our Limiting Beliefs control us. It should be the other way around.

But isn't it exciting to imagine what could be next? What will our grandchildren see and experience? Each of these amazing innovations started out as somebody's dream—a thought no one could see. I'm sure people called the inventors crazy at one point. I am sure many inventors heard people say, "That's impossible!" But inventors create something out of nothing because they imagine they can.

So imagining is an essential first step towards creating a new you and your Totally Fulfilled life.

Core Attribute #5

Totally Fulfilled People have rich imaginations and are able to visualize their future and then take the appropriate steps to achieve their goal.

You have greatness inside of you, just like the people who thought of the fax machine and the Internet. Everyone has imagined something and then seen it become a reality, even you! Perhaps you wished to date someone and then he or she became your spouse. Or maybe you wished for a better job and got one. Those things didn't happen by luck. You pictured it. You imagined it. And then you took steps to make it happen.

We'll utilize that same process together but at a new level. We are going to knock down the walls so your dreams come true, not by luck, but by simple proven strategies that work. We can make each day exciting because you will be taking the right steps towards your dreams and not allowing anything to steer you off your path to Total Fulfillment.

The Law of Manifestation

There is a principle that many Eastern religions have called the Law of Manifestation. Manifestation is just a big word that means to make real. The belief is that if you have a desire or goal in your mind, it has a certain energy level. The belief is that all life in the universe is just energy working at different levels. If you keep that goal strictly in your mind, you're working at a lower level of energy. The theory claims that since it's contained inside your own head, the energy doesn't flow as freely.

The thinking goes that you should let your thought out and release that energy into the world. Pretty simple really. How many times have you mentioned an idea to someone, and they told you that they knew someone else

> *...you should let your thought out and release that energy into the world.*

who was thinking about the same problem and came up with a solution that you could try yourself. Remember the story of my shoulder? That's a simple example of how manifestation works. If I hadn't said anything, I may not have heard of that alternative to surgery. Putting the thought (energy) out there attracted a similar kind of thought / energy.

It works in larger ways too.

Dan's Story

I have a friend who was working in the marketing department of a large company. Dan was satisfied with that job, but not Totally Fulfilled. He was a passionate photographer and he loved to travel and shoot lots of pictures. He gave them away to friends, and everyone told him he was so talented he should sell them to magazines.

He'd been discouraged from pursuing a college art degree by his parents. They thought he'd wind up one of those starving artist types. They preached safety and security—don't take chances with your future. So when people told Dan he was good, he didn't really believe them. He thought they were just being nice. Eventually, he heard that from enough people that he thought they were being honest and that he did have a really good eye.

One day at work, Dan was talking with a client. The client was saying how he was satisfied with the marketing pieces the company was doing for him, but he was never happy with the graphics—particularly the photos. Dan had been having a particularly frustrating day, and he was surprised to hear himself say,

"You know, I've done a lot of photography work myself. If you ever need someone for an assignment let me know." Dan and the client then talked about Dan's travel experiences, and the client asked him to email some of them to him.

Dan did as asked but didn't hear back from his client and soon forgot about the conversation. A month later, Dan picked up the phone at work. It was a call from a local branch of a travel agency. They were putting together a brochure and needed someone with photos of beach and mountain locations in the US. They'd heard through a friend that Dan was a good photographer and they'd seen some of his work. Could he put together a portfolio and have it sent over?

Dan was thrilled. He sent the pictures over to the agency. Eventually, they bought several of his existing shots and asked him if he could go on location to a new Mexican resort on the Yucatan to do some more shots. Dan managed to get the vacation time off from work and did the shoot.

Now, three years later as a result of opening his mouth to his client, he's represented by a top photo agency. He no longer works in the marketing department, and supports himself and his new wife as a freelance travel photographer. He is doing what he was meant to do, what makes his heart feel passion because he voiced that was what he wanted for himself.

Dan wasn't lucky, he didn't have all kinds of connections, he simply let it be known what he really wanted out of life, and the universe took over. He didn't just let his dreams ponder in his head, he voiced them, took action and got results.

He managed to get over those negative assumptions and Limiting Beliefs that held him back. But it all started with that simple first step—from Thought to Action.

Chapter Check

❑ Our imagination is a powerful tool for creating a new reality for ourselves.

❑ Many of us have lost our child-like ability to pretend.

❑ Visualizing your future is a way to re-fire our imagination.

❑ All of the greatest innovations in our life-time started as a thought.

❑ Making our desires and goals known can help us attain them.

❑ Totally Fulfilled people have powerful imaginations, can visualize their new reality, and take the action steps needed to make their thoughts real.

Chapter 6

No More Obstacles

"Opportunity is like a well.
If you don't lower the water bucket,
then all you get is dirt."
—Doug Firebaugh

A few years ago, I lived in upstate New York in a tiny little town. Next door to where I lived was roughly 30 acres for sale that an older farmer had. The area was filled with apple orchards and grape vineyards. It was a beautiful part of the country. I wanted to buy this property, but at the time I didn't have any cash, hence obstacle number one. I faced a couple of extra obstacles as well as just lack of funds.

An older farmer owned the property, he was a wonderful man, but he also had a set price in mind for the property and would not budge. He had the property for sale for several years and had a number of offers, but he wanted his exact dollar or he wasn't selling it. That was just that. The property was slightly overpriced but that did not matter, because I saw the long term value. So that was obstacle number two.

The third obstacle was that there were several neighbors who did not want that property developed. Did you ever hear the phrase, "Not in my back yard"? Well, that thirty acres was the backyard of quite a few people, some of whom were dead set against it being developed. I was a member of the town's planning board, so I saw that kind of thinking a lot.

Theirs was a natural reaction, in fact, I've felt that way myself. But this was an extreme case of not in my back yard. Unhappy neighbors with an agenda to stop development is not a good thing for anyone. You can't stop development if it is by the book, legal and allowable in the area, but it can surely be delayed and be very costly.

So I had three major obstacles. No money, the guy wouldn't budge on his price, and I knew the neighbors were going to fight me. Obstacles that may be enough to turn most people away and not get the rewards I ended up receiving.

The first thing I did was go to the gentleman who owned the property. I said "I would love to buy your property". His response was, "I can't budge on the price". I said I knew that and I was prepared to pay full price. The price of the property at that time was $180,000. He was excited about that. I said, you've had it for sale for almost two years and you still have no money in your pocket. Correct?"

I continued, "How about we do this? I will give you $180,000—100 percent of your asking price." He was excited.

Then I said, "But here's what I would like to present you in lieu of you getting full price. I would like to give you $90,000 now, and I want to give you $90,000 a year from now with no interest. You can hold the mortgage on the property, and if I sell any part of it, you get 50% of those proceeds until I am paid in full with you or the complete balance in one year whatever comes first. Does that work for you?" In two minutes he said yes. Obstacle number one was overcome.

Now, the second part, a little bigger obstacle was that I had no money. At the time I was fortunate enough to know a gentleman who had saved up a bit of money that was making him minimal interest sitting in the bank.

I went to him and said, "Listen, I found a piece of property where I think we can make an absolute fortune". This is a guy who works seventy hours a week to earn the money he had. He didn't know the secrets I did. I said, "Listen, I'll protect you. I'll put the property in your name until it's paid off, and once that happens than we can put it in both our names. You put up the first $90,000, and I do everything else. You don't even have to look at the property if you don't want to. I do all the work, within a year you'll have your money back and I'll pay the 50 percent owed to the seller from the money I generate from the property. Is that a fair deal?" I did everything to protect him. He agreed. So now I got over the second obstacle. I closed on the property using his money and none of my own.

Then there was just one last obstacle. I hate confrontation and I hate when people are upset by something that is inevitable. If I didn't develop that property someone else was going to. So there had to be a solution that would make everyone happy.

This is where thinking outside the box and focusing on the solution keeps your eye on the beneficial result. I wanted to sub-divide this property and make money while at the same time not making everyone in the neighborhood upset.

In past cases I had seen that people would hire an attorney and spend the money to fight the neighbors. I looked at it very differently. Instead of hiring an attorney I knocked on the first neighbor's door. I said, "Hi, how are you doing? I'm Dean Graziosi. I bought the property next door." And the first person looked at me defensively. I said, "I'm not here to get into an argument. Here's why I'm here. Development is inevitable. The property is going to be developed some day, so here's how we can go about it. You and I and the whole neighborhood can fight about it and in two years it's still going to happen, and we've both spent a whole bunch of money and wasted energy. Or we could try to find something that makes everybody happy right now. I think there has to be a solution." Taking the high road gave me what I wanted, and I learned something so incredible that it sticks with me even today.

By communicating with the neighbor I found out what everybody wanted—they just wanted a piece of land or a cushion to give space between them and the possible new development. So I sold a cushion to 4 neighbors and took in about $200,000 within several months. I sold each of them the size piece they desired at a huge discount, yet I still made money and we ended up both being happy. I took that $200,000, paid back the gentleman who put his money in, took my half, and paid the $90k I owed.

I hadn't spent a dime of my own money on the property yet, and I was profitable on it already—. But it became ten times better. I went on to sub-dividing the property selling some lots and then eventually selling the sub-division. I ended up taking in a total of around $900,000 from that one piece of property.

Anything you set your mind to is possible…

Do you see why I told you this story? There are so many lessons you can learn from this one simple example. Anything you set your mind to is possible—if you set it in your mind that you're going to do it and just make it happen. I told you that story to show you that we all face huge obstacles. Opportunities seem to find people who are willing to go for it—while others stand on the sidelines wondering, "What happened?" You create your own luck. The harder you work on you, and creating a "core" for success, the more luck you find.

When successful people hit a brick wall on their journey towards a new accomplishment, instead of turning around, they have the ability to find a way through it, over it, and around it and continue their journey. It's the kind of person who understands that the Universe sees fit to reward us with what we ask of it. You can become the person who realizes, on the other side of that brick wall could be that pot of

Persistence is the ability to go, even though it seems everything is saying no.

gold, could be that $5,000 a week instead of $500 a week. That same person realizes, that on the other side of the wall there could be another two brick walls. The winner in life is the one who keeps going even when life does not immediately go as planned. Persistence is a great quality. Persistence is the ability to go, even though it seems everything is saying no.

We have learned the power of imagination and that it is the start of everything. So what's next? If you are anything like me, right after you have focused on your dreams, it seems an obstacle pops up in your mind and puts the brakes on your dream. That is the point at which so many people stop, turn around, and accept a life of mediocrity. They do their "somes." They hope by some chance someday somehow somebody will make it better. And unfortunately, in most cases it never does.

Taking on Challenges

What if I told you that, by the end of this section, we could turn your personal obstacles—no matter what they are—into challenges you will be excited to overcome? We grow when challenged. We are evolving creatures, and as we grow and fix one issue, two more will pop up. Overcoming temporary setbacks and obstacles, especially in times of uncertainty and adversity, brings out the best in us. You're about to learn the tools to defend your mind from feeling desperate, helpless, and incapable when you approach challenges allowing yourself instead to change and know that anything is possible.

So let's take a minute and go back to why you have this book in your hands. My guess is that you have things in your life you want to improve. In fact, you've read this far, so you're committed to go to a whole new level and reaching your full potential. This is not about eliminating problems in your life, because that will never happen. This is about how to deal with problems as they arise and what to focus on at that time.

Eliminating Excuses

What would you love to accomplish, overcome, change, or create? What's wrong in your life presently? If you compare your vision of a Totally Fulfilled life to your life right now, how do the two differ? What scares you, gives you that knot in your stomach, or causes you fear, anxiety, stress, and hopelessness? Are finances your biggest stress? Your health? Your weight? Your relationships? Depression? No matter what our obstacles are, we need to address them, overcome them, and find out why they hold you back.

Be extremely honest with yourself here. What obstacles popped into your head when you were trying to dream of that perfect life? Think what they were, and we'll come back to them in a minute.

This may seem a little unsympathetic, but your obstacles may be nothing more than excuses that you have created without realizing it.

I can almost hear you right now: "Yeah, but, you don't understand. I can't even begin to imagine my dreams, because _____ (fill in the blank with the "limit")." Or maybe you're saying, "That would be great. But I have four kids. I'm already working two jobs. There's no way around my obstacles."

I have felt and said the same types of things at many points in my life, especially when someone was trying to give helpful advice. As real and painful as my past obstacles were, I also know I have invented some pretty good excuses over the years that delayed my progress and evolution to a better me.

Now, I believe the greatest failure is letting an excuse stop me. You can't make a new life for yourself and have excuses at the same time. You have complete control of what an obstacle means and how you handle it. Say this phrase out loud: "If it's to be, it's up to me." Do it one more time. "If it's to be, it's up to me."

> *I believe the greatest failure is letting an excuse stop me.*

My life changed forever when I learned how to break through most if not all of my obstacles. Think of how amazing it would feel to have the skills and confidence to know that no matter what came up, you had a way to resolve it immediately. I wish I would have learned ten years ago that obstacles really are nothing more than excuses. Unfortunately, at that point I didn't have the tools to overcome them. Now, we both do.

So, what were the obstacles in your life that popped up and brought you back down to your current reality?

Are the obstacles the same ones that have held you back from so many other opportunities in life?

Is there just one big one?

Are there three or four or maybe even ten different ones? Try to keep them in a bigger category, meaning if your car is a piece of junk and breaks down all the time, and you can't make it to work, then that may be the need for more money.

Realize that obstacles may be right in front of you that you have just grown accustomed to. For example, maybe you finally just gave in to the fact that your boss would never give you a promotion, and that is now a part of your life; you *accept* the position, disappointment, and lack of fulfillment at work. In this case, what is your obstacle? Is it your boss? Is it that you are afraid to make a move? Is it your limiting beliefs holding you back? Is it your family because you feel you need to provide for them even if you sacrifice your life to do it? Is it your spouse, your education, your finances?

Really dig in deep, and be honest. Find your personal obstacles and whatever stops you from tearing them down to get what you deserve. Remember, there are no wrong answers.

Core Attribute #6

Totally fulfilled people are responsible. They don't make excuses, they make things happen and don't let things happen.

Face the Fire

I hope you can write down your obstacles, but if you can't right now, at least focus on them in your mind.

We can encounter dozens and dozens of obstacles; however, we can classify most under a few main categories.

◆ *Having limiting beliefs*—This one is so important that I dedicated the first section of this book to it. If any of your obstacles fall in that category, you can use the skills you have learned in those chapters to recognize them and change them to limitless beliefs.

◆ *Fear of failure*

◆ *Fear of not having enough time to make a change*

◆ *Fear of not having enough money*—or the belief that "It takes money to make money." This is a huge one for people who want to make a lot of money.

The last big obstacle we will address is "change." Change is such a big one that I dedicated the next section of the book to it.

Don't Fear Failure

Let's start by saying, "Without failure, there is no such thing as success." Write that down on paper, on your hand, or maybe even on your forehead if you have to.

I'm kidding about the forehead.

"Without failure, there is no such thing as success."

But I am very serious when I say, "Failure is part of success." Think of it this way: You're driving down a road for the first time, come to a fork in the road, and make a left turn. You get terribly lost and realize you should have turned right. Guess what? Every time you come to that same fork in the road, you will never make that left again. You learned a lesson. That's what life is about—it's a bunch of left and right turns. If you try something and you fail, you have learned a lesson and will never make that mistake again.

...allow mistakes to be a positive force in your life.

People who are afraid to try never get those lessons and never sharpen their skills to make a difference in their life. Failure gives you the opportunity to learn from your mistakes and propel you on the next thing you try. You need to alter your thinking to allow mistakes to be a *positive* force in your life.

To do this you just need to change the associations your mind makes. If you associate failure with hopelessness, disappointment, or insecurity, then failure will always hold you back. But if you change that association and connect failure to gaining courage, learning lessons, or creating building blocks to a new life, then failure becomes a virtue, a positive instead of a negative.

Now, I am not saying that you should *try* to fail. I want you to succeed in everything you do. I am also not saying you need to be the happiest person on earth after you fail. That's unrealistic. But I *am* saying that if you are ready to make a move towards a

79

better life, disappointment and failures *will* happen as you move from where you are to where you want to be.

Can you now see how failure could be one of the foundations of your success? That's a lot different than what you thought of failure just a few minutes ago. Do you see how failure could help you learn which way **not to go**?

Winston Churchill once said, "The definition of success is going from failure to failure without losing your enthusiasm."

I love that saying; it's one of my favorites because it reinforces what I've come to believe: all the failures that you think are the end of your life are really nothing more than a lesson. I've made disastrous decisions that I thought devastated me, but I looked back later and thanked God I learned the lesson from that poor choice. I wouldn't be the person I am if that experience didn't happen to me.

Here's one last, powerful exercise. When your fear pops up, simply ask yourself: "What has fear cost me to this point in life?" Answer honestly. What could you be doing right now if you hadn't been overtaken by fear of failure in the past? I'd bet you'd probably be further ahead. I know I would be, but we can't do anything about yesterday, so let's start doing something today.

Giving Up is Not the Definition of Success

By the mid 1990's, I had already accomplished a lot in my life, considering where I came from. I had an auto sales business, and I owned and managed eighteen apartments. I worked every day fixing and selling cars and most nights I renovated apartments and managed the ones I owned. At that time, the Internet was new, and a few associates and I created a company that worked on new ideas for supplying information, services, and products online to create residual income.

Through a stroke of luck, I got Tommy Lee and Pamela Anderson's e-mail address. I sent them a short, polite e-mail telling them that I had created a system that, combined with their star power, could create a web site that could have tens of thousands of monthly subscribers paying a monthly fee of $19.95.

I hoped to hear from them but honestly never thought I would. To my surprise, a few days later I got an email from Tommy Lee saying, "Give my attorney, David Rudich, a call because we are interested." I was so excited my limbs were shaking.

I wondered if I had what it took to communicate with someone on David's level. To my surprise, I spoke with an amazingly kind and polite man who invited me to Los Angeles to discuss a deal.

Nervous and excited, I met with David and was very honest about my background. I told him my follow-through and vision for the future was as good as anyone twice my age or someone with a college degree. To my surprise, my age and education didn't seem to matter to David. His main concerns were his clients' welfare, the profit potential, and that our idea sounded like a great opportunity for them. He called Pamela, told her he liked the idea, and thought we should pursue it. In fact, he suggested we all have dinner that night.

As you can imagine, I left that office on a high I had never felt up until that point, at least in my business life. I wasn't dressed as sharply as most people. I didn't have a college degree, and I was in my mid-twenties. But I was judged by my ideas, vision, and honesty and nothing else. I headed back to the room waiting for a call from David about a meeting with Tommy and Pamela.

Well, the meeting didn't happen that night, and David scheduled another meeting the following day with me, himself, and Tommy and Pamela's accountant. It was a totally different meeting than the one the previous day. Immediately, I knew I was not being judged for my idea, my intentions, and the money we all could make, but for my look, and my lack of schooling and experience. The accountant even asked how I got a meeting with David in the first place.

My confidence was flushed down the toilet in a matter of minutes. The accountant informed me that there would be no meeting with Pamela and Tommy until he went through our business plan completely. I knew in that instant that the deal and the possibility to show what I could do and how much money we could make were over, at least with me being involved.

I now look back with gratitude since I was able to grow from this experience!

Just the day before, I'd felt ecstatic, and now I left feeling lower than I ever had before. I was angry with myself for not handling the situation better. I was totally upset with myself because I felt like I was out of my league and should have not tried to reach a level higher than I was supposed to. Even as I write this now, I can feel the same knot in my stomach I had then, but I now look back with gratitude since I was able to grow from this experience!

So I went back home with my tail between my legs, feeling like a victim. What's worse, as soon as I got home, my pager went off, and it was one of my tenants, whose plumbing backed up, and there was literally six inches of raw sewage in the bathroom. No plumber would clean it up, so I got fishing waders and did it myself. As I was cleaning, I remember saying, "Back to reality."

When this event happened, I was still learning about all the techniques I am now able to share with you in this book. I was not thankful for what I had already accomplished. I was *focusing on what I didn't get and how I had failed.* My limiting beliefs that were deep inside of me were coming out strong. I couldn't possibly see how this failure could be a lesson at that time.

Looking back, I realize this was a huge turning point in my life. After a few weeks of misery, I woke up one morning and snapped out of it. I started thinking of everything I had already accomplished, my amazing family and friends, and the love I had in my life. I was not going to let one deal or one man's opinion of me or my ideas change my desire for more—my desire to grow. I deserved more, and I was going to continue, and somehow, someday, I knew this would be an incredible lesson.

I thank God for this failure now. It *could* have stopped me in my tracks, and I would have lived a mediocre life. It *could* have instilled a strong limiting belief in me that if I try something and it doesn't work out, or if it hurts me, I should never try again. And that might have extended to anything in my life: relationships, health, emotions, business, and everything in between.

This story is an example of the type of failures that led to my success. I may not have gotten that deal, but I probably was not ready for it at the time, and losing it only made me stronger and smarter for the next one. Today, I am fortunate enough to make more money than I ever dreamed possible, and looking back, I know that would have never have been possible without failures and lessons like this one.

Chapter Check

❑ We all have to face obstacles on our journey to success.

❑ Totally Fulfilled people always manage to find a way around, over, or through the brick walls we encounter.

❑ You must take full responsibility for your life—excuses are not allowed.

❑ Failure is not something to fear but to learn from.

❑ Lack of time is not an excuse.

❑ Lack of money is not an excuse.

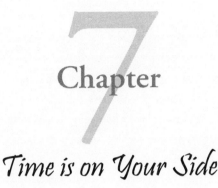

Chapter 7

Time is on Your Side

*"I don't know what tomorrow will bring—
except old age and death—
but I do know that I do have today,
one absolutely glorious day that I will savor
and make the most of as if it were my last one...
because it may be!"*
—Gary Fenchuk

Did you determine "lack of time" to be an obstacle in your life? Almost daily, I hear people say, "I just don't have enough time." They have no time for self-improvement. No time for better health. No time to work on their passion. No time to find the right partner. No time to spend with their kids. No time to make extra money or get ahead. Did you ever hear the saying, "I'm too busy making a living to get rich?"

Time is not an obstacle. Lack of time is just a huge excuse. Time is *not* an obstacle. If you are like most of us, you are *wasting* time in your life right now on things that don't benefit you, your love life, your family, your income, or your health.

Assess Accurately

Anything that doesn't make you truly feel good inside or that does not benefit you or the people you love the most is a waste of your time, and I'm positive you could find five to twelve hours a week that you're wasting. Wouldn't it be incredible to focus that time on something that could change your entire life, something that could give you money, a better relationship, a better feeling about you?

I know you have heard the saying "Work smarter, not harder." After you complete this book, that old expression won't be just a phrase but an intrinsic part of the way you live, think, and breathe.

If you really want something and you say time is a problem, then maybe you really don't want it as much as you think you do. If you want more out of life, you know it's not going to happen on its own. There is no magic box that's going to pour out money. There is no pill that will make you skinny. There is no fairy dust to make your relationships better. So you need to set aside time to make your dreams happen. Four hours a week or forty, as long as you say that you really want to change your life and live differently, then you can find the time.

How? If we're honest with ourselves, every one of us could find five hours a week that we're doing something non-productive or foolish. Maybe instead of going out with the guys after work a few nights a week, you only do it a few nights a month. Instead of going to the mall every Saturday, you can do it one Saturday a month. Here's a major source of wasted time: How much time do you spend each hour, day, and week on negative thoughts?

Take a few minutes, be honest with yourself, and write down or think about time in your life that you allocate to things that do not reward you, your future, or the people you care about? Find it and let's use it for something so much more fulfilling.

Core Attribute #7

Totally Fulfilled people are productive and focused. They are able to accurately assess what's important to them and to achieving their goals.

Sometimes I know I use this as an excuse when one part of my life is slipping. I've said, "I just have so much going on, I can't handle that part," when I was temporarily overwhelmed or overloaded. But then I use the same methods I am teaching you to overcome these feelings and stop allowing myself to use lack of time as an excuse.

I run several companies, travel a lot for business, and have a number of major responsibilities that eat up almost every minute of every day. God has given us all an equal 24 hours in a day. It's what we *choose* to do with that time that makes the difference.

Setting Your Priorities

My schedule does not allow me to watch much TV, but I try to watch one show on Sunday night that really touches my heart. Extreme Makeover—Home Edition helps families in need get a new house, and it has evolved to doing so much more for people. Sometimes when I am thinking my life is so hectic, so busy, maybe even feeling that my pressures are so much greater than the average person's, I see a story like I did the other night, and it brings me right back to reality.

A brave fireman saved a medic's life during a shoot out. The story of his bravery alone touched my heart, but that was only the beginning of the story. He was a single dad who worked two other jobs to support his three kids. As if things were not tough enough, his youngest son's best friends were brothers in foster care who were to be separated. This amazing man, with all of life's obstacles in front of him—mostly time—adopted these two teenage boys and took them in as his own without question or complaint. Through it all, you could see in his eyes the fulfillment and joy he experienced from being a great dad, a great fireman, and a great person.

This man overcame obstacles *as they came up* by focusing on the outcome. It was an amazing story and gratifying to see him get a new home and help for his children to go to college. But something tells me that even if this show had not come into his life, he and his family would have been okay. This man eliminated excuses, especially lack of time, and just got things done. And so can you.

…there is nothing anyone else out there can do that you can't do…

Remember, there is nothing anyone else out there can do that you can't do, whether your level of adversity is higher or lower than the man whose story I just told you. Whatever it is, you can overcome it with the right tools.

Crazy as it may sound, so many people will get my book, get really excited after reading the first few pages, but not go back to it because they think they don't have the time to finish it. They'll inevitably go back to the life that they are not completely happy with in the first place. But that's not *you*. So how could time stop a person like *you*? It can't!

Do this for yourself: Take the next week of your life and keep a journal of what eats up your day. Find the time you need to allow yourself to make these changes in your life. Prioritize and possibly eliminate something else to fit "You" into your schedule.

If you are always giving to other people, you eventually won't have anything left to give. On the other hand, if you are empowered, confident, and fulfilled, what you can give to others will be ten times stronger.

Chapter Check

❑ We all have the same amount of time in any given day.

❑ We choose how we spend that time.

❑ It is important to assess accurately what matters most and spend our time accordingly.

❑ Focusing on your priorities eliminates the feeling of being overwhelmed.

❑ Totally Fulfilled people are productive.

Chapter 8

You Don't Need Money to Make Money

*"Your living is determined not so much
by what life brings you
as by the attitude you bring to life;
not so much by what happens to you
as by the way your mind looks at what happens."*
—Lewis L. Dunnington

So many people want to make it big. They want to go one hundred steps up the financial ladder in minutes. But they surely have an obstacle in their head about why they can't. Why? Because they believe they need money to make money! As you saw in the previous chapter, I was able to make an extremely profitable real estate deal without using any of my own money initially. So, let's throw that obstacle out the window.

As you know, my parents divorced when I was young and we struggled financially. I hated it when we moved into a trailer, drove a beater of a car, and we couldn't afford the clothes all the other kids were wearing. Growing up wanting and needing things made me want to be a success. Growing up, I grew vegetables at my Gram's house, and sold them at a local farmer's market. I then started holding garage sales. I would clean out a neighbor's garage for free and then sell what they considered "junk." In 7th grade I would buy Hubba Bubba bubble gum for twenty-five cents a pack and then sell individual pieces to other kids in the cafeteria for a quarter. I knew that hot lunch cost seventy-five cents and most of them would have a quarter left over. Later on in high school, I cut down trees and sold the firewood by the cord. Some of the same kids who had made fun of me were now my employees.

I started with a lot of ideas and a willingness to take action.

I've been able to be as successful as I have not because I started with a lot of money. Instead, I started with a lot of ideas and a willingness to take action.

Many of my best students who have made a lot of money started without using their own money. I have made a fortune in a variety of ways without using a dime of my own money; rather, my desire fueled the success.

If I used lack of money as an excuse I would still be fixing cars for a living. I'm not saying fixing cars is a bad way to make money, but I wanted more, as I am sure you do, too. You can change your financial destiny and make an absolute fortune starting with little or no money. You need to be in the game and not just sit around talking about it.

Most likely you don't have a rich uncle or family member who is going to leave you millions. Learning the secrets of working with no money can seem like a challenge. But really it's like everything else in this book. Once you have the right core attributes, anything you plug into it is possible.

What if, as of today, you said, "I now realize there are millions of self-made millionaires who started with nothing. They dug inside themselves to find the answers and they succeeded. There is nothing anyone else can do that I can't do." Just saying that out loud is empowering. Through necessity and practice, I have mastered a few unique techniques to make money without using any of my own. It's amazing what you can create out of necessity or when you want something bad enough. Do you want it?

The Power of Desire

Let me give you a quick story of something I did as a kid that bought me my first really nice fishing pole and a beautiful Shimano reel at a little sporting goods store down the road from my grandmother's house. We certainly didn't have the money to buy a fancy fishing pole. But I didn't feel sorry for myself. Instead, I tried to find a way to get that rod and reel.

For almost an entire summer of Saturdays, I had yard sales. I went to my grandmother and Aunt Hazel and Uncle Bud and a few of my grandmother's friends and asked them for anything they didn't want anymore or I cleaned out their garages for free. I got ton's of stuff for my garage sales, much of it probably garbage to them, but at the end of the summer with the money from that so called garbage, I bought that rod and reel. I still have that fishing pole today.

In order to play and do it big, you have to be able to do it small. Money does not have to be an issue; it's a measurement of value—how much do you want it? I have seen my students make more money in a week without using their own money, than they had made working all year in a job they hated. They wanted it; I simply supplied the blueprints.

This book is about creating a core inside yourself that will allow you to succeed in *every* area of your life. And if making more money is one of those areas for you, then go at it with everything you have inside of you.

...go at it with everything you have inside of you.

Recipes For Financial Independence

I have been fortunate enough to work and be extremely successful in many fields, as I have shared with you. I have made money selling bubble gum, having yard sales, selling firewood, cars, real estate, doing writing and consulting, and more. And with the lessons I learned doing those things, plus possessing a core for success similar to what we are building in this book, I have learned ways to make more money faster and easier, starting with little or no money, by working smarter, not harder. And there is no reason you can't do the same things I have done.

I love to talk about money! I could literally write an entire book on strategies for true financial independence starting with little or no money. But, for right now, I want to share some simple truths that will help you on your path towards Total Fulfillment, especially if making more money is one of your desires.

The money you earn is in direct proportion to the value you bring to others, plain and simple. But value does not have to mean long hours and hard work, if you approach it correctly. As you earn money, you can use money to make even more money. Most people work their whole lives to earn money; few ever really figure out how to *make money work for them.*

Pay Yourself First

Here is a simple lesson to remember; get control of your money. If you make $500, $1,000, $5,000, $50,000 or $500,000 per month, **pay yourself** 10% minimum to put towards building freedom first. So many people pay everyone else and then live on what's left over. Seems like a pretty sad way to live life, don't you think? Make it a habit. Find a way to put 10% towards your future. You are worth it!

Here's a simple example of the payoff you'll get. Let's say you take just $30 dollars a month—$1 a day—and your goal is a million dollars. What does the average person do? They put their money in a traditional bank that pays 2-4% returns. Maybe they put it in a CD or something. At just $30 per month at 3% interest (which is likely lower than inflation), you'd earn a million dollars after about 150 years.

Invest Wisely and Often

On the other hand, if you took the same $30 per month and found a way to get at least 10% interest compounded, you would have a million dollars in less than 60 years.

This is where you need to take action and look for things like mutual funds. *Mutual funds* are simply a collection of funds, typically groupings of company stocks, bonds, and financial instruments that diversify your money for optimal growth and minimal risk. A money manager oversees and manages the variety of funds purchased and sold for their members.

Good mutual funds have been around for ten years or more, have consistent track records, and show long term averages of 10% or greater. You simply deposit your money into the account, and you have the opportunity to benefit from compounded interest. If

I were starting from scratch, I would set up a mutual fund account right away.

You can invest in a mutual fund through an IRA (Individual Retirement Account). There are many advantages to having an IRA. Talk to a financial advisor or go online and learn about the different options available and how to maximize your tax deductions and contributions.

Use the Magic of Compound Interest

Did you know that if you take a penny and double it every day, at day twenty-eight, you'll have over $1 million dollars? That's the magic of compounding returns.

Want to see something fun? If you take the same $30 per month and find a way to get a 20% return of interest compounded, you would have over a million dollars in just under 35 years. From personal experience, I can confidently say that, with smart buying, you can earn a 20% return on your money and more through smart real estate investing.

I have been making tremendous returns on my money for over eighteen years with real estate. And from personal experience, thinking a little differently than most people, and seeing my students all over the country do it, proven techniques exist to make huge profits without using any money of your own.

If real estate excites you, I suggest you find a mentor or someone who is already making money with real estate and latch on to him or her. You can also read a lot of great books out there that can help as well. Of course, I am partial to my "Think A Little Different" real estate course that you can check out at *www.totallyfulfilled.com*. It has helped people all over the country reach tremendous financial success.

Remember this important point: Find a way to put your money into something that pays at least a 10% return. Even if you are starting with a minimal amount each month, get started. Once you develop the habit, increase the amount you put into your investments. What if you put $60 per month? $100 per month? Or even $200 per month?

As a parent, you could set up an account for your kids and literally put them in a position to be *multi-millionaires in their thirties*! Wouldn't that be great? Or you could create a trust fund and let it ride for fifty or sixty years and end up with millions or even billions of dollars? We're talking Rockefeller money. And leaving a legacy you can be proud of, because you were smart and took action *now*.

The key is to get started. Regardless of your situation, look at all possibilities. I'm not giving any financial or legal advice here, but I want you to understand that there are many options for you to consider, even if you do not have a lot of money to invest.

> *Regardless of your situation, look at all possibilities.*

Building Wealth

To overcome thinking that you need money to make money, you need to know the difference between *linear* and *passive income*. With linear income, you work for an hour, and you get paid for working an hour. With passive income, you basically do something once, and get paid over and over again.

Linear income is basically what most people in the world do. This is typically the type of income that most of us go to school for. We get a good job when our adult life begins. Once in a linear job or business setting, you may realize that there is not much room for growth. And many people, once they are in their linear 9 to 5 job, realize that it is not what they truly want, and it does not fulfill them.

Passive income is derived from finding a way to create something once that you can sell over and over. Of course, passive income is what we all strive for but most people do not know where to begin. What's great about passive income is that with a little *outside the box thinking*, you can discover many ways to create this with little or no money of your own.

Core Attribute #8

Totally Fulfilled people are money-wise. They value money for the freedom it brings them, they invest wisely, enjoy what they have, and let their money work for them so they can alleviate the stress from lack of money in their current life and leave behind a legacy.

This type of income can snowball on its own without you having to monitor it on a daily basis. For example, if you decided to create a monthly electronic online newsletter about how to stay healthy, you could write one each month with maybe a day's work and sell that one piece of information over and over again with a click of a mouse. You could potentially have thousands of people enjoying your service, getting great value, and paying you monthly for something you did once: Minimal cost, minimal effort, with great upside profit potential.

This is just one example of thousands of opportunities you can create. Do you currently own a business and have a database of satisfied customers? Offer them a monthly newsletter or service that can help them, while you increase the value of your company or product, and at the same time create passive income for yourself. Want to start your own business? Try to implement a passive income model into your plan.

This strategy is not something new, and it can be adapted to many different fields and industries. Bill O'Reilly, of Fox News Channel's *The O'Reilly Factor,* is a great example. Love him or hate him, his TV news talk show brings in the audience. But what you may not realize is that, in addition to his talk show, he promotes his passive income machine at the end of each show by sending people to his web site. There, he offers a monthly service that has incredible value to his subscribers for just a few dollars each month. The information and services are created once and sold over and over again. So people get tremendous value for minimal cost while Bill O'Reilly and company have the opportunity to receive passive income from potentially millions of people, making money even when they are sleeping. A service like this is a win-win for everyone involved.

With an open mind and some thought, you'll find potential for passive/residual income in most fields. You just have to keep your eyes, ears, and mind open to it.

With the millions of people online each day, the Internet is one of the most incredible ways to build passive income. Visit *www.totallyfulfilled.com* to learn more about this excellent source of income and our Financial Education Courses that can show you how easy it can be.

The Efforts of Many

When you hear someone talk about a successful person, they often refer to doctors or lawyers. I have friends in both professions, and I can tell you that they worked their butts off to get where they are, especially paying for all the school they had to attend. And some are very, very successful, while others do well for themselves, but they are not getting rich. Why? Because doctors and lawyers who do not have their own practice earn only linear income. They work on a certain number of patients or for a certain amount of time and get paid for their services.

There is another way. The super-successful doctors and lawyers who are envied by many have realized what I am about to share with you. They have their own practice or group. So when they are working on a patient or on a case, at the same time they may have five, ten, twenty or even fifty other people working for them, so they're making a small profit off of each of the other people in their practice or group, getting paid through the efforts of others.

This can be the case with almost any organization that is structured correctly.

Share Your Knowledge For Huge Profits

Turn your passions, expertise, and experience into profits. Build the model for success—prove it works, then sell the idea or strategy as a consultant. I do this on a regular basis and get paid a significant amount of money to do it. You too, have skills that, if honed correctly, can translate into a business that makes you money while you help others make money.

> *Turn your passions, expertise, and experience into profits.*

Here is how I approach a consulting job: If I know I can significantly increase the revenue of a company with my proven knowledge or techniques, I find out what their current profit is, and I ask for a royalty based on my results. I will come in and put systems in place that should increase profits. If they do not, I don't get paid, so there is no risk to the company. But if I do increase their revenue, I get a portion of the extra money I bring the company.

For instance, I have a company that I literally put less than 3 week's work into and got paid a royalty of up to $6000 a week for well over a year. Not bad. And the company that was paying me loved sending me the checks because what I did produced about $100,000 a week in sales for them. I did it once and got paid over and over again.

Make Money In the Middle

Many opportunities in the world can allow you to profit by being the "middle man." When I was broke and wanted to make money with cars, I would match up buyers and sellers and make a profit in the middle. I did that with garage sales when I was a kid, and now eBay does it to generate billions of dollars.

Being the "middleman" is a great way to make money without using any money of your own. This method can branch off in many directions to fit your life. If you own your own business, having a middleman (or woman!) to help you expand your business could be extremely beneficial.

If you don't own your own business, your "middleman" services could help expand another person's company while you make money. For example, go to smaller service-related businesses people use every day—car repair shops, plumbers, carpenters, pool cleaners, landscapers, fuel oil distributors—and tell them that you want to print up cards with a special code on them to recommend their services to everyone you know. In return, ask for a small percentage of all sales generated by this form of advertising.

Small businesses especially love advertising that they only have to pay for if they get results. Tell the business owner how much better this referral method of advertising is than an expensive ad with no promise of sales.

Wherever you go and whenever you speak to anyone about anything, you have a list of service places for all of their needs. You are helping these companies get additional business, helping people in need of services with a referral, *and* you are making money in the middle, spending no money of your own! If you own your own business, you can try this same method, in reverse.

Instant Pay Raise

Advancing in a current job is a very real opportunity for some people, so you don't necessarily have to quit your 9 to 5 job to become wealthy. You could possibly implement similar strategies to those you have learned and will learn in this book in your current job, and if they increase the company's profit or sales, you could have the chance to get a promotion and/or a pay raise.

One last thing about your job—even if you dislike it or you know it is temporary—do it as well as you can because you never know what is around the corner. I have hired waiters. I have filled positions in my companies with people in totally unrelated fields who make twice as much as they used to and love their positions. I liked their professionalism and work ethic, even in a difficult or unfulfilling job. Always be your best and good things will come of it.

Open your mind and don't be afraid to think outside the box...

I hope I opened your eyes with these examples of realistic opportunities to make money, whatever your current financial situation. Open your mind and don't be afraid to think outside the box to maximize profits in whatever it is you want to do.

To take your income potential to another level, don't forget:

◆ Create residual/passive income.

◆ Profit from the effort of others.

◆ Use the power of the Web.

◆ Share your knowledge for profit.

◆ Be or use a "middle man."

◆ Take your current job or career to the next level.

Once again, you don't need money to make money. All you need is *you* and the "core" for success we are starting to build. Get excited! Your life is about to change forever!

Chapter Check

❑ It takes effort to make money.

❑ Desire will help you find a way.

❑ Understand and use the power of compound interest to make your money work for you.

❑ Seek ways to take advantage of passive (multiple earning) income and not rely on linear (one time earning) income.

❑ Take advantage of the power of many to spread expenses and increase profits.

❑ Turn your passions, interests, and knowledge into profit centers.

❑ Make money in the middle by bringing buyers and sellers together.

❑ Take your current job to the next level to earn a raise in pay.

❑ Totally Fulfilled people use money wisely and to their advantage.

Chapter 9

The Power of Solutions

"Opportunities multiply as they are seized."
—Suz Tzu

So far in this section, we have covered the importance of your imagination and how all things start as a thought. You imagined what a fulfilled life would be for you. What would make you feel good on the inside? Remember that it's okay to imagine yourself wealthier because money can allow you to feel a certain way. And if handled correctly, money can be a great tool in the journey towards the new you.

We have also discussed changing your beliefs and some other major obstacles like fear of failure, not having enough time to change your life, and the belief that you need money to make money. In each chapter, I hope I not only helped you address these issues but also gave you rock solid ways to achieve and overcome tough obstacles. Having these skills is a must if you want more out of life.

And now, as we head towards the end of this section, I am going to give you three additional techniques that will ensure that obstacles will never hold you back from living a life filled with everything you want.

These additional three tools are:

◆ Taking immediate action.

◆ Focusing on the end result.

◆ Stopping negativity.

Take Action

Without action, knowledge doesn't matter. Knowledge may be power, as the saying goes, but to me, knowledge is useless without action. Knowledge + Action = Results.

If a computer is filled with incredible programs that could change your life, but you never turn it on, or you don't know how to use them, then what's the sense of having the wealth of information in the computer?

The same goes for you and me. If we have this amazing, life-changing information, but we never take action to put the knowledge to work, it can't do anything for us.

...keep your momentum moving forward, towards a solution.

When obstacles pop up, don't let them weigh you down, don't ponder them, and don't let them grow bigger and bigger by avoiding them. *Take action immediately.* Even if you only take the first step to figure out how to overcome an obstacle, keep your momentum moving forward, towards a solution.

Focus on the Finish Line

We must appreciate every step of life's journey. But where obstacles are concerned, a great technique when one bogs you down or changes your plans is to focus on the *outcome* you imagined when you started.

This one is easiest for me to explain with an example from my life. I have wanted to write this book for a long time. When I first thought of writing it several years ago, I realized I wasn't ready yet; I didn't have everything I needed to share with you, as I truly feel I do today. But it started in my imagination. When I thought of writing this book, I imagined how amazing it would feel to be able to help so many people. I imagined this book in the hands of millions of people. I thought of how proud my family would be and the feelings that gave me—the joy of contributing and making a difference. I imagined it with so much intensity that it was like it had already happened.

Yet, since I started writing this book, I have had unexpected obstacles pop up along the way that put me temporarily off-track. I wanted to be done many months ago, and I was hoping to be able to write it in a peaceful environment. But because I own so many businesses, that was temporarily impossible. I couldn't just stop everything and focus on my book completely.

At times I wanted to say, "Forget the book for now. I'm too busy." When that happened, I revisited what I originally imagined, going back to the end result of getting this book done. I remembered the feelings I would have, helping others live a Totally Fulfilled life, and that sparked excitement and desire to keep moving forward all over again.

Don't hesitate to revisit the feeling of the result, when you come up against an obstacle, and don't let *anything* stop you from getting there.

A Picture is Worth a Thousand Words

I want to share with you a powerful tool that a very dear friend shared with me. It can keep you on track in the midst of adversity. Get a wallet-size picture of someone who is very dear to you—your spouse, children, parents, etc. On the back of the photo, write the three biggest obstacles in your life. Remember to put them in the broader categories as we discussed, like *fear of failure, lack of time, and limiting beliefs*. Then I want you to look at the picture. Turn it over. Look at the obstacles. Turn it over. Look at the picture. Turn it back. Repeat this at least five times.

Now, when you're faced with one of these three biggest obstacles, pull out that picture, look at it, and then flip it over. Read the obstacle you're facing out loud. Then flip it back over, and ask yourself out loud, "What's most important to me: letting the obstacle stop me, or the love I have for (the person or people in the picture)?"

This simple strategy could allow you to never look at obstacles the same way again.

These three simple tools can help you find the answers you are looking for to overcome obstacles you encounter. You will train yourself to be a problem solver. You'll handle your obstacles head on. While most people avoid, and even run and hide from their fears, you will possess a secret as powerful as rubbing Aladdin's lamp.

Even if it sounds silly to you right now, say this to yourself or better yet, out loud: "I face my obstacles head on." One more time: "I face my obstacles head on."

Saying things out loud makes a statement to the world. And once you put it out there, it's easier to stand by your words. Say these out loud and see if any of them spark an empowering emotion inside of you. I know they do for me...

◆ "I have found a way to overcome anything that gets in the way of my life of total fulfillment."

◆ "I have the knowledge; now I need to take action."

◆ "I want it, and I'm worth it."

◆ "I'm a great investment."

◆ "I'll make time for me so I have more to give to others."

Repeat the ones that feel good, or create your own, based on what we have covered, and repeat them whenever you need to empower yourself.

Remember, problems and obstacles will always come up. We are not trying to avoid them or falsely hope they will magically go away forever. Rather, we are training ourselves to easily overcome problems with the special skills we have learned in this section. In fact, the better your life gets, the larger the tasks you accomplish, and the more money you make, the bigger the obstacles will become. But once you have the right mindset and core you will arrive at the point where you say, "Bring them on."

Chapter Check

❑ Take immediate action

❑ Focus on the end result

❑ Eliminate negativity

Chapter

Break Through to the Other Side

"The only time you can't afford to fail,
is the last time you try."
—Charles Kettering

The most rewarding feeling in the world is to set a goal, accomplish it, and then watch your life start to change. There's no greater joy than transforming a dream into reality. Set a goal in your mind, and remember that no matter what, you are going to *make it happen*.

I can't tell you how many people I've met who are great starters but poor finishers. It's easy to get excited about things you love, but it takes practice to stay focused and excited when times are tough.

A friend once told me something that has stuck with me for a lifetime. When I was saying how hard a certain job was, he said: "Son, remember in life you are not judged on the things you like to do or are easy to do, but rather on how you deal with the difficult things or things you don't like to do."

...commit to being a "finisher."

No matter what you do in life, whatever you try, whatever you want to accomplish, commit to being a "finisher."

So many people give up just before the finish line. I've seen it happen a thousand times. Remember, winners win because they do what winners do. It's not about working harder, it's about working smarter.

I remember being a teenager and saying that some day I would make $1,000 a week. When I surpassed that and got to $5,000 a week, I said, "Wow, five grand a week. Where could you go from here?" Well, I now have weeks that I make $35,000 and $40,000. I know that many people work an entire year for that. I also know some people work the same amount of time I do for $350 a week.

I simply found a way to build a core that allows me to accomplish anything and overcome any obstacle. If you follow my secrets, you can do what I did in any area of your life: make five times your current income, overcome depression, lose weight, fix a damaged relationship, or end an unhealthy one.

If I didn't take action and use the techniques I am sharing with you, I would still be working on cars. It was only a handful of years ago, I got up every day and worked on cars and run-down apartments. There was absolutely nothing wrong with that profession and working hard physically, but while I was doing that, I was working on my dreams, and I never gave up on them. Let's make sure you never give up on yours either.

The Possibilities are Endless

Before we move on to the next section, take a moment and imagine once again what your ideal life would be. I think you will find one or more things about your picture may have changed.

When you take out obstacles, your dreams seem to reach out further than you may have originally thought were possible. Instead of imagining a raise, now you may be picturing your own business. Instead of a bigger apartment, maybe you're picturing a new home. Instead of hoping to lose a few pounds, now you picture yourself at your ideal weight.

Seriously think about it: How would you like your love life to be, your personal life, your health, your financial goals, your state of mind, the relationship you have with the person closest to you, or the relationship you want to have? Take a moment and try imagining it as if it has already happened. Try to see it. Feel it. Touch it. Taste it. Has it changed? What have you added? What have you expanded? If your eyes are getting wider, wait until you see what's coming next!

Section Summary

- ❑ Our imagination is a powerful tool for creating a new reality for ourselves.

- ❑ Many of us have lost our child-like ability to pretend.

- ❑ Visualizing your future is a way to re-fire our imagination.

- ❑ All of the greatest innovations in our life-time started as a thought.

- ❑ Making our desires and goals known can help us attain them.

- ❑ Totally Fulfilled people have powerful imaginations, can visualize their new reality, and take the action steps needed to make their thoughts real.

- ❑ We all have to face obstacles on our journey to success.

- ❑ Totally Fulfilled people always manage to find a way around, over, or through the brick walls we encounter.

- ❑ You must take full responsibility for your life—excuses are not allowed.

- ❑ Failure is not something to fear but to learn from.

- ❑ Lack of time is not an excuse.

- ❑ Lack of money is not an excuse.

- ❑ Desire will help you find a way.

❑ Understand and use the power of compound interest to make your money work for you.

❑ Seek ways to take advantage of passive (multiple earning) income and not rely on linear (one time earning) income.

❑ Take advantage of the power of many to spread expenses and increase profits.

❑ Turn your passions, interests, and knowledge into profit centers.

❑ Make money in the middle by bringing together buyers and sellers.

❑ Take your current job to the next level to earn a raise in pay.

❑ Totally Fulfilled people use money wisely and to their advantage.

❑ Take immediate action.

❑ Focus on the end result.

❑ Eliminate negativity.

Core Attributes of Totally Fulfilled Individuals:

- ◆ Positive / Optimist
- ◆ Open Minded
- ◆ Passionate
- ◆ Grateful
- ◆ Imaginative
- ◆ Responsible
- ◆ Productive
- ◆ Money-Wise

Part 3

11 Chapter

Choose to Change

"If we don't change, we don't grow.
If we don't grow, we are not really living.
Growth demands a temporary surrender of security."
—Gail Sheehy

Recently, I went to a restaurant nearby that has been in business at the same location for a number of years. The food is good, the décor is ok but nothing special, and the menu hasn't changed for as long as I've been going there. The restaurant was one of the first in an area that is now booming with development. That development brought several new businesses and other restaurants to the area. The development means more traffic and you'd think that would be good for this restaurant and exciting to it's owner.

However, because of how the owner interpreted change in his life, he did not look at it that way. I was at the salad bar and I overheard the owner complaining about the restaurant that opened across the street. They were seeking the city's permission to expand by building an addition. Business must have been good there. The owner of the place where I was eating wasn't happy about the possible expansion, so he hired an attorney to fight it. He was determined to do everything he could to stop it and spend whatever it took to do so. I could hear the anger in his voice, and I felt sorry for him. The man refused to recognize that change is an inevitable and important part of life. This could be perceived as an exciting time for business and personal growth. Yet it was converted into stress, anger, and negativity—none of which are part of a fulfilled life.

Instead of looking at the changes as a threat, he should have seen them as an opportunity for growth

I'm not a cold-hearted person, but I really sat there thinking about how misguided this owner was about change. He had to have been aware that the neighborhood was changing and the businesses and restaurants should have made him think about updating his place. Instead of looking at the changes as a threat, he should have seen them as an opportunity for growth. He was content to stay in the same place, and in life, when you insist on sitting still, someone is going to pass you by. That's just the way it is.

I don't mean that he had to play the game of keeping up with the Joneses—you shouldn't really care what others have—but he should have kept his operation more current, seen what was happening around him, and had some plan for dealing with it. It could be as simple as seeing change coming and embracing it by being prepared with simple, easy-to-apply techniques you will soon learn.

I wanted to say to him, "Why don't you take the money and energy you're spending on a lawyer and use it to update your décor? Do some advertising or some guerilla marketing to the many new offices and businesses around you? Why not build relationships with those people instead of working to get a reputation as an obstacle?"

Using your energy to prevent someone else from growing and changing makes little sense to me. Instead of being envious of their position, why not take that as an opportunity to look at your own situation to see where you might improve?

In the last section, we talked about imagining your Totally Fulfilled life. You discovered that imagining gives you not just an amazing feeling of freedom, but is also the first step to changing your life. We worked on eliminating most of the obstacles that may have been in the way of your success. I hope your imagination expanded from the beginning of the section until the end. Now it's about to expand even further.

In this section, we are going to address change, which freezes many people dead in their tracks. We all face a number of different kinds of change in our life: changes we need to make but are afraid of; unexpected, sometimes devastating, changes; and changes we should have seen coming but ignored.

Would your life be different right now if one of those types of changes hadn't held you back in the past? Or, is one of the changes holding you back right now, and maybe led you to read this book?

By the end of this section, we are going to take to an even higher level that feeling you had when imagining your Totally Fulfilled life. In fact, what you imagined won't be just a wish or a dream anymore; it will be a reality soon to come. You will be able to visualize what you want as if it has already happened.

Make the Commitment

Sound a bit crazy? Give this section 100% of yourself, and you'll see what I mean.

You've imagined what you want; you have broken down many obstacles. Now it's time to commit to change. It starts at the core—your thoughts, beliefs, and actions—to truly get control of dealing with change.

Let's face it, most people hate dealing with change, yet it is the one constant in our lives. We can fight or ignore change, or we can embrace it. If we don't learn specific ways to embrace change, living life at a Totally Fulfilled level is impossible. Not making a change when you know you should, or fearing change, is the fastest way to a stagnant life. Take this journey with me. I'll show you how to embrace and welcome change, no matter how difficult it may be.

A New Beginning

Every emotion is a thought we give life to. Whatever you concentrate on grows. Embracing and welcoming change is no different.

You've probably experienced unwanted change many times already in your life. Have you ever had a relationship that didn't work out? At ten years old, I remember running home and telling my mom, "I'm in love." She shook her head, knowing what had started and, in this instance, what would surely end. She told me that what I felt wasn't love, but I didn't believe her. A few weeks later, the inevitable happened. My girlfriend told me she wanted to be "just friends." Those are words you never want to hear, no matter how old you are.

I remember feeling devastated on the bus ride home. I went to my room, locked my door, put on a Journey album, laid face down on my bed, and cried. And why shouldn't I? My life was over, wasn't it?

Can you remember a similar experience? That intense sadness lasted a couple of days. Then I just seemed to recover without much effort. Before I knew it, the feeling was gone and I was back to being a regular kid again—at least until the next girlfriend. I forgot about the unhappy ending and found a new love. Even though at the time I thought the breakup was the worst thing that could ever happen to me, I got over it and moved on.

Sure, it hurt, but I didn't throw gas on the fire. I didn't feed the emotion. As a result, it went away. Our youth can sometimes teach us our greatest lessons. I was too young to know to fear change, so I moved on without serious side effects. But as an adult, change got tougher and tougher until I learned to embrace it. That is when my life changed forever.

Most change seems to work this way. When we move from one situation to another, initially it's scary or challenging, and ultimately our condition gets better if we're willing to detach ourselves

> *If we embrace change, we are on the way to a Totally Fulfilled life.*

from the situation. It isn't always easy, but it's worth it. If we embrace change, we are on the way to a Totally Fulfilled life.

If change was not a factor, or you had no fears in your life, where would you be today? More important, where would you go from here?

When a business associate of mine found out I was writing this book, he emailed me this story from author and business expert Brian Tracy.

> *"A woman in her mid-thirties was married with three kids. Like so many people, she had grown up in a home where her family ridiculed, constantly criticized, and treated her unfairly. She developed a deep feeling of insecurity and low self-esteem. She was shy, quiet, and self-conscious. She detached from any goals and from most people, and had minimal, if any, talent to speak of. She was destined for a life of mediocrity because that was all she was taught and all she expected of herself.*
>
> *"One day as she was driving to the store, a car went through a red light and smashed into her. When she awoke, she was in the hospital with a concussion and memory loss. She could speak, but had no memory of her past. She suffered from complete amnesia. At first, the doctors thought it was temporary. Weeks went by, though, and her memory did not return.*

"The doctors unfortunately did not have an answer. Eventually, she went home with her mind completely blank. Determined to understand what happened, she committed to reading and studying everything she could about her situation. She even wrote a paper about it and delivered a presentation at a medical convention.

"During this time, she reinvented herself, truly becoming a new person. All the support, love, and attention she received made her feel special and valuable. The medical community's attention increased her sense of self-worth even more. She became a positive, confident, outgoing woman in high demand as a speaker and an authority in the medical profession. She turned tragedy into triumph. She lost her limiting beliefs, overcame the fear of change, and turned her fears and obstacles into her greatest strengths."

Powerful!

You don't have to wait for tragedy to turn into triumph. You can make the change today.

It's your choice. This incredible lady made a choice to live life to the fullest—to go for it! Amnesia was the beginning of her change. Why shouldn't the lessons you are learning in this book be the beginning of *your* new life? You are worth it.

It is Never Too Late

On the other hand, my dad has made different choices by not making many changes until very recently. I've watched him do things year after year that caused him pain, sadness, frustration, and added stress. My dad primarily focused on the problem he was facing, not on the solution. When he needed to make a change to get out of a rut, or to advance to a better place, he would revert back to what he knew. As a result, his life remained the same, problems and all. Even worse, he would wonder why he still had the problems, even though, from my perspective, it was so obvious.

But he was not ready for lasting change. He had moments when he was, but only when *others* made him feel temporarily fulfilled. His inner peace and happiness was 100% dependent on other people— a disaster waiting to happen.

I realized early in life that my dad was haunted by a terrible childhood of physical and mental abuse. These events left him with scars he was unaware of and set so many limiting beliefs in him. He was fearful, frustrated, and had poor decision-making skills. No one had shown him another way, until I did my best to let him see the different path his future could take. By then, he had so many years of practicing life the wrong way, it was hard to even give him advice on the possibilities for a right way.

Core Attribute #9

Totally Fulfilled people are flexible—they understand that some changes are inevitable, some they can see on the horizon and prepare for, and others will surprise them. No matter the kind of change, they adapt and grow and not retreat and wither.

I learned a lot of great things from my dad, some of which were what *not* to do.

I know this may sound funny, but I've tried to set a good example with my dad. I've tried to help him make a change, sometimes without letting him know I was planting seeds in his head, hoping they would grow.

I like using simple analogies, and one I often repeat to my dad is, "Dad, it's like being in a canoe paddling upstream. You're trying to get to a destination, yet you hit a section of the stream where you can't move. You paddle and paddle every day but have no luck. All I ask is that you try another route because this one is not allowing you to advance. Try changing your approach. Try going to another part of the stream. You might hit another tough current, but unless you try, you will never know. The fact is, the section you are in is not working."

Doesn't this happen to all of us? We want change so badly, but fear of change and the unknown holds us back from even trying. Are *you* stuck in a strong current, unable to move forward, yet are afraid to try another section of the stream? You have to move, and you have to look forward. I know this is much easier said than done, but the tools to make that move are soon to come.

Realize that you are going to have to move your hypothetical canoe to another section of the stream and at least try a new area. I am not saying you have to yell out "woooooaaaaah" and go full blast across the stream. Simply start the movement and focus on paddling to a new area. If you stay in that current and keep paddling and going nowhere, you'll eventually get tired and give up and then the inevitable happens: you go backwards.

My dad is now experiencing a new life at almost 70 years old, and it warms my heart to see it. It is never too late to reinvent yourself. I am so proud of him for taking action and changing a lot of his limiting beliefs and overcoming his obstacles. His change from just two years ago is like night and day. Now that he's living these success principles, I know my dad would do anything to go back 50 years and practice the things I am teaching you today. Don't wait another day or for another time in your life to make a change—make it now.

> *Remind yourself that the definition of insanity is doing the same thing over and over again expecting a different result.*

Remind yourself that the definition of insanity is doing the same thing over and over again expecting a different result. If what you are currently doing does not satisfy you in all areas of your life, then you must make a change.

Change may appear to be scary and uncomfortable, but think of what these things mean to you: independence, passionate love, financial freedom, accomplishments, confidence, comfort, joy, being stress free, happiness, purpose, strength, health, peace, appreciation, giving, and other words that reflect powerful emotions. You can't experience these feelings if you are unwilling to make a change in your life.

Let's continue this journey so you can learn to embrace change, look forward to it, and await its new, exciting, and different outcome. Even if it is baby steps, it's time for you to MAKE A CHANGE!

Chapter Check

❑ Change is part of the natural order of life.

❑ Anticipate that there will be unexpected changes.

❑ Push yourself to make changes you know are necessary.

❑ Some people would rather experience the pain of the familiar than face the unknown.

❑ You can change at any time and at any age.

❑ Change does not equal loss—it can lead you to better things.

❑ Totally Fulfilled people are flexible and they welcome and anticipate change as an important part of life.

Chapter 12

Let Go of Your Fear

"There is a law in psychology that if you form a picture in your mind of what you would like to be, and you keep and hold that picture there long enough, you will soon become exactly as you have been thinking."
—William James

Let's really dig in and address what change can do for your life, how to recognize when you need change, and how to make it something exciting, not frightening.

As a whole, change can seem huge and difficult to overcome. But break it down, and it can be a piece of cake. There are all types of change, but most of them can fit in the two main categories:

1. Change you see coming

2. Unexpected change

Decide what kind of change you are going to make before it decides for you.

The first kind of change, that which you see coming, requires you to be observant. You can see change coming in many instances, so don't turn a blind eye, hoping it will go away, because in most cases it won't. Decide what kind of change you are going to make before it decides *for* you.

For example, let's say your company is downsizing. You are getting nervous and should be *doing* something, but you're not. You're paralyzed with the thought of starting anew. You have worked hard and deserve this job, though it looks like you are going to lose it anyway.

You can handle this situation two totally different ways. Which way are *you* more likely to handle it? Which way is more productive and advantageous for a Totally Fulfilled life?

1. You could go to work bitter, scared, stressed, nervous, and insecure every day, wondering where your future lies. As you do this, you will jump fully into the "Why Me?" syndrome: trying to figure out who is to blame; spending energy just wishing things could go back to the way they were; waiting to be laid off; and getting angrier and more insecure all the time. You're letting outside influences direct your thoughts, your life, and your future. *You are waiting to react to a change.*

2. You could take the opposite approach and *control the events that affect your life.* You could take a moment, and look back at all the good that came out of your current job. Maybe you met new friends, had new experiences, and learned from mistakes you made. You certainly learned what *not* to do in business. You could be thankful that you had this job up until that point when so many people around the world only wish for a job. You could embrace and look forward to change and the possibilities that change would bring you, imagining what your ideal

job would be. You could think of who to give your résumé to, maybe even consider starting your own business now. You could lock on to what you've imagined for yourself and focus all your energy on reaching that end result. You wouldn't waste any time, not even a second, trying to figure out who was at fault or why this always happens to you.

How would this approach differ from the first? It's night and day!

Focus on the solution or outcome, not the obstacle, change, or problem.

Doing this is the number one reason for the success I have had in my life to this point. Focus on the solution and don't waste energy on anything else.

> *Focus on the solution or outcome, not the obstacle, change, or problem.*

My grandmother, Carmella Post, had a saying that has lasted me a lifetime, and helps me even more the older and wiser I get: "Don't waste energy on things you can't change—just focus on the ones you can."

Take a second and think what change in your life is coming that you know you should make a move on. If you do not move on it, it will direct you to make moves out of desperation. If you take the initiative to change something before it changes on its own, then *you* are the one in control. But if you ignore it until it slaps you in the face, then you will be *reacting* to a problem.

If you had no fear of change, then would you start small changes today? I bet you're saying yes! Fear of the unknown may be holding you back, but *you are already a master of dealing with change*. You've been doing it your entire life. You just need to step it up to another level.

Have the confidence to know you can do it now. Become a person who focuses on outcomes and accomplishments. Focus on the solution when a problem occurs and focus on the incredible outcome that can result from change. Remind yourself that if you don't make a change, one thing is for sure: your life will remain exactly as it is today.

In the small town I grew up in, a lot of people worked at IBM. Years back they had a big layoff. I remember customers at the local deli were very nervous, wondering if they were next. It was a great lesson for me at a young age. I heard the same phrases almost everyone uses: "How could they do this to me? What am I going to do now? The management stinks! This is unfair!" Yet, I remember one IBM employee asking another if he was nervous about losing his job and the second guy said, "You know, I needed the change. Working at IBM taught me a great deal, they are a great company, and I was treated well, but I have always wanted to have my own consulting business, and this may be the kick I needed to start it. What I've learned at IBM makes me feel confident that I can succeed. So instead of sitting around waiting to get laid off, I'm going to resign and start my new venture."

He was the only one I saw who had a different way of thinking and embraced change. He had a different walk, a different smile, and a different level of confidence. He was facing the same impending change issue as everyone else, yet he chose to give it a different meaning. He took action first, remaining in control rather than the opposite. I don't know if he succeeded, but I know he looked at the change as a positive thing and was ready to embrace his future even though he was not totally sure what it was. He looked towards a better future and did not harp on the loss. I wanted to model my own outlook on his.

Core Attribute #10

Totally Fulfilled people actively take control of their lives and the changes that are a natural part of living. They don't simply passively respond to change.

In life, there are two types of people: thermostats and thermometers. Thermometer people go up and down, up and down, being influenced by all the external factors in their life. It doesn't take much effort to react; most people wear their attitude on their sleeve, reacting to the circumstances *happening to them.*

The people who make it really big are those who are like a thermostat. *They* control the temperature. *They* control their environment. They *respond* to situations, not react to them. It takes effort and discipline to control our thoughts and ultimately respond to situations. You are what you think you are, most of the time.

What if you could be so powerful that you could not just *control* change, but you could also alter its *meaning* in your life? What if, instead of your mind telling you that change meant pain or fear, you could train your mind to look at change as exciting, new, and leading to something better?

Wouldn't it be great if the thought of change instantly meant the chance for something better, something you used to dream of, an opportunity for a more fulfilled life? That the word "change" actually made you smile or even laugh out loud?

Once you conquer the fear, you'll realize that change equals only two things:

1. Something better for my family or me.

2. A valuable lesson to learn from. In the worst case, you eliminate an area not to try again.

What's the worst thing that can happen when you make a change? You could fail. But remember the phrase you learned in a previous section: "Failure, mistakes, and problems are part of success."

In fact, during an interview, Thomas J. Watson, the founder of IBM said, "If you want to be successful faster, you must double your rate of failure. Success lies on the far side of failure."

Modify the meaning of "change" in your mind, eliminate the fear, and it will be something you look forward to, because something better could be just around the corner waiting for you.

Chapter Check

❑ Some people are like thermometers—they passively reflect what is going on in their lives.

❑ Some people are like thermostats—they actively control what is going on in their lives.

❑ Be a thermostat—take control of change and alter its meaning in your life from something to fear to something to welcome.

❑ Change can mean something better for your family and you or it will provide a valuable lesson to learn from.

❑ Totally Fulfilled people are active controllers of their life and make changes and not just respond to them.

Chapter 13

Embrace the Unknown

"Twenty years from now you will be more disappointed
by the things you didn't do than by the ones you did do.
So throw off the bowlines.
Sail away from the safe harbor.
Catch the trade winds in your sails.
Explore. Dream. Discover."
—Author Unknown

Bill Murphy, my friend and father-in-law for 10 years, went to the doctor one day feeling fine, only to find out a few weeks later that he had lymphoma cancer throughout his body.

No one could ever be sure how they would handle such an extreme unexpected change until they were faced with it. Bill had always been a structured, persistent, strong person, but cancer with a high terminal percentage presented with no warning? Well,

Bill reinforced everything I believe in by not wasting even a day asking how or why this could have happened to him, and he didn't look for anything or anyone to blame. He simply set his mind on the outcome of getting over it and never looked back. He decided to give this unexpected change in his life a different meaning.

Bill was seemingly unshaken and spoke with an unexpected air of confidence. He told me he was going to beat the cancer no matter what he had heard about the disease. He had already figured out his ideal outcome and was starting the steps to fulfill it.

By the grace of God, at that time I was doing some consulting work for a leading health expert who specialized in strengthening immune systems through natural remedies. So I told Bill I would do my part to find realistic, researched, and proven ways to help him stay strong, especially since he had already decided to start chemotherapy right away because the cancer was in a very advanced stage. At that point there was nothing else I could do. He had already set his mind on the end result of being cancer-free, and that was the start he needed.

I did a lot of research and shared what I learned with Bill about boosting his immune system. Bill endured twelve weeks of chemotherapy and despite weight loss, discoloration of his skin, aches and pains, loss of his hair and appetite, and minimal sleep, he never missed one day's work. I am so thankful to say that today he has been totally cancer-free for over a year. In fact, he just recently went back for a test, and he is in perfect health.

How did Bill make this miracle happen? First, instead of wasting his energy on why or how this happened to him, he took the knowledge I shared with him, and the information he learned on his own, and made the necessary changes in his life for optimal results. Second, he embraced the unexpected change and focused on the outcome from the very start.

Please know that I am not saying that all cancer can be cured by focus and wheat grass. But I watched this happen with Bill first-hand, and I have to share this amazing story with you. If you know someone who is sick, or if you are sick, do your best to give yourself no other option but to *get better*. Focus on how you are going to feel or look when you beat the disease and you have recovered. Put pictures up around the house of when you looked your best and visualize the day you will be looking that way again. What you focus on is what you are. Giving up, feeling like a victim, or wasting time on "poor me" takes away energy that must be focused on the optimal outcome. Learn all you can about your situation, figure out the best result for you, take action, and fight it all the way.

> *What you focus on is what you are.*

Unexpected change can be terrifying. In the previous chapter, we talked about change you could see coming, like your company downsizing. Unexpected change is getting fired for no apparent reason. Instead of seeing your relationship taking a bad turn, your spouse comes home one night and wants a divorce. Or maybe you find that a friend or business partner took advantage of you, and it devastates your finances or trust. All changes can be devastating, even more so when they are unexpected and maybe even life-threatening.

In most cases, we overanalyze the situation and ask ourselves the wrong questions, like "How could this happen to me?" "Why did this happen to me?" and "Who is to blame?" We waste energy on worry instead of using it to find a solution.

> *"What's the use of worry? What good does it do?*
> *Does it add a single thing to our life? Of course not.*
> *And if worry can't do such things as that,*
> *why worry over bigger things?"*
> —Corinthians

Don't waste time trying to figure out why this happened to you, or who is to blame, or why you didn't deserve this. You probably didn't deserve it, but the fact is change is still going to happen.

What if as soon as unexpected change happened, you immediately asked yourself these powerful, solution-oriented questions?

1. *What happened?* Describe it in detail. Write it down.

2. *What, if anything, can I learn from this so I can avoid it in the future?*

3. *What would be the ideal new outcome to this unexpected change?* Write it down.

4. *How can I start* today *to make this hopeful new outcome a reality?*

It's so important to eliminate the "victim" questions. Focus on *these* questions, which will empower you. Focus on a positive outcome, even if this unexpected change steered you in a new direction. Embrace that new direction, appreciate the past for what it has taught you, and take hold of your future.

Enjoy the Benefits Before They Even Happen

To immediately help you deal with change, expected or unexpected, first envision the ideal scenario for after the change happens. Where would you be? In a new job? Healthy? In a new relationship? A *better* relationship? Getting a raise? Starting your own business? Building a better relationship with God or a Higher Power? Where could you be?

A few times a day, *imagine it has already happened*. Let yourself feel that your change produced the results you'd hoped for, and enjoy that image for a few moments. Turn off the cell phone. Do it while the kids are asleep. Whenever you have a quick moment, trick yourself into believing the change has already happened and see what that feels like. Everything starts with a thought and a feeling.

Remember, *you* are what you focus on. If you focus on the negative of the change, you will experience fear. If you can use the techniques in this section, along with focusing on the outcome of the ideal accomplishment of your change, then all your energy will go in the right direction.

Chapter Check

❑ Unexpected change will come your way.

❑ Focus on outcomes and solutions and not on why something happened to you.

❑ Embrace the new direction your life has taken and use your energy to steer the best course forward.

❑ Envision the best after change scenario to help you focus and direct your efforts.

❑ Totally Fulfilled people anticipate that unexpected change will happen and remain flexible.

Chapter 14

Change the Association — Change Your Life

"Our self image and our habits tend to go together. Change one and you will automatically change the other."
—Dr. Maxwell Maltz

I have helped people start a new business, make more money, fix a relationship, re-arrange their finances, get a promotion at their current job, quit smoking, exercise on a regular basis, and eat healthier, all by sharing simple techniques I use in my everyday life. In many cases I did nothing more than help them eliminate the fear of change. They already had everything else it took to reach their goals, as I am sure you do.

I want to share one more piece of the "change" puzzle that can ensure that fear of change will never stop you from going where you want to go, and that is by changing the association of what change means to you.

The best way I can describe what I mean about changing the association is to relate it to something that happens in many people's lives. Even if you don't have any bad habits or addictions, the gift you can give someone else from the tips in this section are powerful and proven to support a healthy lifestyle.

Breaking a habit, starting a good one, or ending an addiction can all happen when you change the association of what that thing means to you.

Let me give you an example of someone I helped quit smoking. A young lady of 26 had been smoking since high school, just like her mother and grandmother had. She said she wanted to quit, but found it hard because, she said, "I gain weight when I try to quit, and I get headaches. Besides, smoking helps ease stress for me." I remember wanting to yell out, "Relieves stress! You're right. It relieves stress because it may kill you!"

But I would never say that because I knew that, at that point, those were truly her beliefs and associations about smoking. Tobacco is one of the most addictive drugs on the planet. So many people who smoke attach certain meanings to it, whether those meanings are true or not. This young lady had associated smoking to being thin, no headaches, and a relief of stress. Her association to cigarettes was all good for continuing smoking and all bad for quitting.

I didn't lecture her at all. I just said, "Even though you brush it off, I know you are aware that smoking causes death. And typically it's not a pleasant death, right? So, let's say 25 years from now, you are in the hospital, dying of lung cancer. In pain. Tubes up your nose. I.V. in your arm, and gasping for air. Your family is around, and they don't want you to go. As harsh as it sounds, can you picture it?"

She said, "Yes."

"What if a genie appeared at your bed side and granted you one wish? What would that wish be?"

She immediately replied, "To live!"

"Okay," I said. "Well, guess what? Rewind 25 years, and you can grant that wish to yourself *right now*."

I could tell I hit a nerve. Now that she was open to it, I went on to briefly explain to her that, in her mind, she had linked smoking to good things and quitting to bad things. All she had to do was to associate different things with both.

What if, instead of your current thoughts, you attached smoking to having smelly breath, hair, and hands. Even worse, you were ignoring a serious health issue that you knew was killing you?

If you quit, you could be a role model for others. You can be around to see your family, your children and your children's children. You have a greater chance of living a longer, healthier life. You would be in control of your decisions. You could feel good that you are looking after the 50-year-old version of you.

To quit would mean more happiness, the opportunity to learn a *new* way to deal with any stress, to exercise and eat right for optimal weight, to walk up stairs without being winded, and to be proud of yourself. What's more important to you? Sucking on a butt, or living your life?

> *It's all about changing the associations we have with anything we want to change, quit, or start.*

It's all about changing the associations we have with anything we want to change, quit, or start. If you change the meaning, you can break the habit. In the case of a habit or addiction, you can trick your mind into realizing that the painful part is *continuing* the habit, and stopping will bring you pleasure. That is all your mind needs to quit. This "change the association" tool applies to any change you want to make. Associate positive things and outcomes with what needs to be changed and negative associations with things staying as they are.

Before I was done with her, I said, "Okay. Really fast, write down ten benefits to you and the people around you of quitting smoking." She wrote them down in a minute. Then I said, "Now quickly write down five things that benefit you and people around you if you continue to smoke." She didn't write one. And no one could, if they were being honest with themselves.

Again, this technique can apply to *anything* in your life, not just an addiction or habit. I am using the example of this young lady and smoking because she never thought in a million years she could quit. She had already tried a patch, gum, and even hypnosis.

I'm not sure which part of our discussion made her quit, but she has never smoked again.

We kid ourselves into attaching good feelings and happy thoughts to our addictions or current unpleasant situations we may be in. We can fool ourselves into believing it's okay to continue what we are doing, even if it is life-threatening. If everyone else I'm around is doing it, it must not be that bad, right? How else could someone allow himself to believe it's okay to overeat, drink excessively, do drugs, gamble, smoke and other things that destroy people's lives?

When I was young, my grandmother and I were watching a show where kids were doing drugs. She said something to me like, "As you go through life, look at all the people who do drugs, and see if you can ever find one truly great thing that came of it."

Will you ever hear that a drug addict was such a success and had a great family life? Or will you hear how he lost his home, his business, and his family? When something has so much negative effect on so many people, why would it miraculously be great for you? My grandmother taught me the power of association, and I didn't even know it!

If you have a habit, addiction, or something that is hurting you, and want to break free from it, then practice the exercises above to change the association and what it means to you. Create the proper associations with pain for continuing, and let your body and soul realize the benefits of stopping. Be honest to yourself and give the problem its correct meaning. Soon you'll develop a new pattern, one that supports your quest for massive success in all areas of life.

Chapter Check

❑ Understanding the power of associations is a key to dealing with change in your life.

❑ Your associations are your thoughts.

❑ You have to change your thoughts to change your actions.

❑ Changing your actions will change your life.

❑ Change your associations to change your life.

Chapter 15

Whatever It Takes

*"It's the constant and determined effort
that breaks down all resistance
and sweeps away all obstacles."*
—Claude M. Bristol

It's easier to get wealthy and live a Totally Fulfilled life than it is to get by and make a living. Sound strange? Well, it's true, because you don't have much competition. So few people are willing to even try to be Totally Fulfilled. I have been lucky enough to learn that it just takes a little extra effort to get extraordinary results.

Part of the reason we created our Protégé and Mentor Program was to help work directly with our students and make them accountable for change. We give people the tools for massive success. But sometimes we all need a little push to *use* those tools and take action.

If *you* ever need a little push, then find a mentor or coach who can help keep you on track. Tiger Woods has a coach.

Michael Jordan had a coach. If you can't find one, go to our web site, *www.totallyfulfilled.com* and learn how you can. Chat at no charge with an advisor about what can help you stay on track. Whatever it is you need to do, take action and make that change you need to make.

I get many emails from students in our program. Commonly, they ask, "Dean, what is the biggest thing I need in order to get started making money in real estate? Do I need a lot of money? What would you say the most important part is? Is it getting my real estate license? Should I work with a 'no money down' deal, or should I go with tax sales?"

...make a change in your life and take action right away.

My answer to most is simply this: "I think the number one thing is making the conscious decision that you are going to make a change in your life and take action right away. Follow through no matter what tries to stop you. You must make the conscious decision and say, 'I'm going to do this no matter what. I'm going to get through to my accomplishment. I'm a 'whatever it takes' kind of person.'"

Are you a "whatever it takes" kind of person? I have absolutely no doubt that you *can* reach a level of life most people just fantasize about. Why do you think shows like "Lifestyles of the Rich and Famous" and "Cribs" are so successful? Because most people just *wish* they could have a better life, so they see it through other people's accomplishments. But they never take one chance in their life or take action to make it happen for themselves. Unfortunately, most just talk about it, or even worse, they hit one obstacle and turn back to a comfortable but so-so life.

Get uncomfortable. Be unsatisfied and say it out loud if you have to. It's a great step towards making a change, because no one likes to be uncomfortable.

Wouldn't it be great to have the confidence to call yourself a "whatever it takes" kind of person and then have others say that about you, too? How would you like to be at your office, at home with your kids, or at a high school reunion and hear someone say about you, "He (or she) is a 'whatever it takes' kind of person. He (or she) made a change, overcame obstacles, and is now living an amazing life."

This can start in an instant. Next time you walk by a mirror, look at yourself and say, "Starting today, I am a 'whatever it takes' kind of person. I will never stop growing and achieving." Every time you look in a mirror, while washing your hands throughout the day, wink at yourself and smile, because you have a new secret—a new theory about yourself. Just thinking about it feels good, doesn't it? Imagine when it starts taking place.

It Can Last a Lifetime

In order for things to change, you must be willing to change. Be willing to schedule a change in your life and look forward to it with open arms as something new, with endless opportunities.

- ◆ Don't hope it'll happen.
- ● Don't just dream about it.
- ● Don't just wish it were going to happen.

Schedule the change in your life. Stay focused on your goal and make it happen.

At a seminar once, I asked, "How many people in the room would love to be a millionaire?" Just about everyone raised a hand.

Then I asked, "How many of you have an idea or strategy to become a millionaire?" More than half the hands in the room went down.

The next question got most of them: "How many of you are actually making the necessary changes in your life and working on your way to becoming a millionaire?" That's when almost all the hands went down.

Folks, it's not going to happen on its own. Whether you want to be a millionaire, be healthier, love on a deeper level, or lose weight, it's all the same. These actions and tools for learning are the keys to creating a core for success that will allow Total Fulfillment in all areas.

Handle things as successful, fulfilled people do and you will get the same results. In order to get a Totally Fulfilled life, it's great to think it. It's great to wish it. But *it can only happen if you schedule change and take action to make it happen.*

Take Your Dreams to Another Level

As we end this section, take a minute and really think about what we have done so far and how it may already be allowing you to set higher goals or allow you to dream on another level. Accomplishing incredible goals or fulfilling your wildest dreams is not for other people, it's for *all of us* if we take the action to make it happen. We've worked on turning limited beliefs into limitless, empowering beliefs, and we've worked on your ability to truly overcome obstacles that may be holding you back from a life you deserve. Now what if you added to the mix that you are *not afraid of change*? Use what you just learned to make change something that you *need* to do and are *excited* to do, because it can lead you to a life that is Totally Fulfilled. We are on our way!

Chapter Check

❑ Consciously choose to make a change and take action immediately.

❑ Don't just dream—do.

❑ Even the smallest of steps everyday in a new direction will give you the momentum you need.

❑ Schedule change and take action to make it happen.

Section Summary

❑ Change is part of the natural order of life.

❑ Anticipate that there will be unexpected changes.

❑ Push yourself to make changes you know are necessary.

❑ Some people would rather experience the pain of the familiar than face the unknown.

❑ You can change at any time and at any age.

❑ Change does not equal loss—it can lead you to better things.

❑ Totally Fulfilled people are flexible and they welcome and anticipate change as an important part of life.

❑ Some people are like thermometers—they passively reflect what is going on in their lives.

❑ Some people are like thermostats—they actively control what is going on in their lives.

❑ Be a thermostat—take control of change and alter its meaning in your life from something to fear to something to welcome.

❑ Change can mean something better for your family and you or it will provide a valuable lesson to learn from.

❑ Totally Fulfilled people are active controllers of their life; they make changes and do not just respond to them.

❑ Unexpected change will come your way.

❑ Focus on outcomes and solutions and not on why something happened to you.

❑ Embrace the new direction your life has taken and use your energy to steer the best course forward.

❑ Envision the best after change scenario to help you focus and direct your efforts.

❑ Totally Fulfilled people anticipate that unexpected change will happen and remain flexible.

❑ Understanding the power of associations is a key to dealing with change in your life.

❑ Your associations are your thoughts.

❑ You have to change your thoughts to change your actions.

❑ Changing your actions will change your life.

❑ Change your associations to change your life.

❑ Consciously choose to make a change and take action immediately.

❑ Don't just dream—do.

❑ Even the smallest of steps everyday in a new direction will give you the momentum you need.

❑ Schedule change and take action to make it happen.

Part 4

Chapter 16

Make the Connection

"Treat everyone you meet as though they're the
most important person you'll meet that day."
—Roger Dawson

I was on the phone the other day with a business associate. We were both traveling, so we were on our cell phones. I was driving back from the airport and he was on line at the check-in counter. In the background, I could hear flight announcements, bits of other conversations, and an occasional break up in our connection.

We were trying to schedule a meeting and set an agenda, so we both trying to refer to our calendars to figure out what dates would work for each of us. A pretty typical business communication, right? Well, in the middle of the call, he got to the head of the line. All along I had been asking him if it would be better if I called him back. He kept insisting it wasn't a problem—he can multitask with the best of them. I could tell he was distracted, and our conversation was mixed up with his trying to get listed for stand-by on this flight. Frustrating for me, for him, for the gate agent who was trying to help him. I thought we had everything settled, but two days later, I got a call from him. It seems the date we'd settled on, now wouldn't work for him. He hadn't realized he was already booked that day. In the meantime, I'd already had three other people clear their schedules, arrange flights and rooms to be there for the original date of the meeting.

I'm not trying to pin the entire blame on him; after all, I could have said, "Listen, you're breaking up, you've got several other things going on, let's touch base when you get the flight issue resolved." Instead, like him, I wanted to get this meeting scheduled and to move on to the next item on my to do list. How many times have you let a distraction prevent you from communicating clearly with someone else? This was only a business meeting and can be rescheduled, no major harm done.

> *How many times have you judged, compromised, or hurt an important relationship due to lack of or proper communication?*

How many times have you judged, compromised, or hurt an important relationship due to lack of proper communication? We hear so often through life that communication is the key to good relationships—personal and professional. Why do we so often forget that point? Is that the only key to a good relationship?

In order for me to give you everything you need to succeed on a level you desire and deserve, I need to share with you the importance of relationships and communication. I don't just mean relationships and communication with your spouse or children, but with everyone you come in contact with, from a loved one to a business partner to strangers to clients and everyone in between.

For most people, relationships have sparked the best and worst experiences in life. Think about some amazing moments that relationships have brought you. Maybe it's an experience with your spouse, children, parents, or best friend. Maybe it's a moment you shared with a co-worker or boss. Now, I am sure you could also think of some negative responses these relationships may have brought you, such as the loss of a spouse or loved one, the pain of a fight with your children or parents, or the betrayal you may have felt from a co-worker or partner.

Relationships are a vital part of life. How you cultivate them is a key factor in a fulfilled life. Without strong, caring, respectful, and mutually beneficial relationships, you will never reach a level of fulfillment you desire. Fortunately, a few simple approaches to relationships can make them less mysterious. Whether you want better skills to successfully start a new relationship, strengthen an existing one, or assemble the facts to make a decision to possibly end a bad relationship, the information in this section will allow you to make relationships one of the most fulfilling parts of your life.

Just like the main theme of this book is to create a core that allows you to master any part of your life that you choose, establishing a sub-core for relationships will allow you to handle all personal interactions in a manner that produces optimal results. It doesn't matter if you're trying to build a relationship with your spouse or your postal carrier. Each of those relationships should have the same core aspects that will make them successful.

This section will cover all areas of relationships. We are going to cover some things that you probably would never even think fall under this type of category. Remember, we are building a core for success in all relationships, so apply what you learn here to those relationships that will help fuel your life.

My Experience Equals Your Rewards

In my never-ending quest to improve every facet of my life, I have learned specific skills to form bonding, fulfilling relationships. I've also modeled myself after successful people and how they handle relationships. Just as important, I have learned from people with tragic relationships what *not* to do.

Realize that I didn't dream up these techniques while I was sitting on the beach one day. Rather, as I said in the introduction, I have lived more, tried more, failed more, succeeded more, and heard I was crazy more than most people ever do. So that means I got to experience a lot more of life in a shorter period of time, and while doing it I was able to retain so much wisdom on what works and what does not.

I have been fortunate enough to have some of the most amazing relationships a person can have. I have experienced love for another so strong that I would gladly give up my life for them. I have experienced heights of passion that far outweigh what they write about in romance novels. I have shared friendships with unconditional love and balance. I have had relationships with business partners, mentors, employees, and protégés that have graced my life in ways that I could never place a monetary value on. And I have learned from each and every one of these experiences and seen the value they gave my life.

But I have also failed in relationships—some in a big way—that have taught me priceless lessons on what *not* to do. I share this with you because I think it is imperative that you learn from someone who has experienced both sides of the fence and learned from both, rather than someone preaching a theory of one side or the other.

So with my personal experience and by modeling others, I have done my best to lay out a simple formula for success in all relationships in all areas of your life and on all levels.

Good Relationships Begin with Honest Communication with Yourself

The quality of your relationships with your spouse, children, business associates, and even strangers are critical for achieving long-term success. Most people who talk about relationships focus only on what the other person wants, what to look for in a relationship, or what to look for in another person. All of that is very important, but it's missing a big step.

All relationships start with you. You need to know what truly makes you happy, because a relationship can be a bandage for covering issues that may actually hurt or end your relationship. Does that make sense?

The quality of your relationships with your spouse, children, business associates, and even strangers are critical for achieving long-term success.

I have a friend who is only happy when he is in a relationship. It has been a cycle I have watched for years. He never took the time to find out what truly makes him happy in his own life; therefore, he can not know what would make him happy in a relationship, much less what he wants in another person. So he gets into one romantic relationship after another. The bliss of the new relationship keeps him on a high for a while. I will even watch him temporarily take on some of the characteristics of the person he is dating. Then, once things get more serious, he feels they don't have that much in common, and slowly the bliss ends and the relationship fades away. He really does not know why this happens, except that he feels he keeps getting in failed relationships. He blames it on bad luck.

It's not bad luck. Rather, he is going into a relationship blinded by the craving to not be alone, which we all have. But the way he does it makes it a catch-22. He does not want to be alone, so he grabs onto the first person that takes the feeling of loneliness away. But since he really does not know what he wants for himself and in a relationship, he is destined to be alone yet again. Recently, he asked me for advice on relationships. We had a great talk, and today he has become a happier person with himself because he looked deeper in to what makes him happy. The only way to make another person happy is to be true to yourself.

Whether you are hoping for a new relationship or want to enrich a current one, you can follow an easy process so that your relationships can be incredible assets and not chores. This particular section is geared for personal relationships, but since we're building a core foundation, you can use the principles in any kind of relationship. Start this short journey by answering a few simple questions. Your answers may open your eyes to the start of a Totally Fulfilled relationship.

Let's start with you.

♦ What makes you happy?

♦ What emotions do you like to feel on a regular basis?

♦ What activities do you like to do?

♦ What are your plans for your future?

♦ What are your plans for your family? Friends? Health? Exercise?

♦ Is there anything else that makes you feel good as a person?

Now let's think or write down characteristics of your ideal partner in a relationship.

♦ Would he or she be honest? Confident? Caring? Affection-ate? Playful? Strong? Charismatic? Secure? Outgoing? Shy?

♦ What would he or she look like?

♦ How would he or she act on a regular basis?

♦ How would he or she act when a problem occurred?

Then what type of things would this person be willing to give to you?

♦ Would he or she love you unconditionally, take care of you when you are sick, and listen to you when you may be sad?

♦ Would he or she laugh at your jokes?

♦ Would this person be faithful to you?

♦ Would he or she stand by you and stick up for you?

♦ Would he or she take care of him or herself physically?

◆ Would this person support your dreams? Be a great parent?

◆ Would he or she appreciate what you do?

◆ What would you love in a relationship?

Now here is the simple part.

◆ Are you that person you described?

Once you know what makes you happy, you can describe your ideal partner. Then you can make a list of what you would like the other person to do for you. Now it's easy to see if you can get what you hope for. Are you that type of person? Are you the type to give all you would hope to receive?

If you are in a relationship and you are looking for someone to listen to you when you are upset, are you able to listen in return? If you're looking for your spouse to stay fit, are you staying fit? If you're looking for appreciation for your hard work, are you doing the same? If you can't give back what you want from the relationship, it'll never be a totally fulfilling relationship. And if you are going into a relationship, start with these things in mind. Start the relationship as the person you plan on being through the entire relationship. Have you heard the term "bait and switch"? So many people start the relationship as a totally different person than who they really are. Inevitably, the true you comes out. So why not start out that way and avoid the headache down the road?

This is the foundation—the core—of what makes a healthy relationship. And with a strong core, you can build anything on any level. And these core factors relate to productive business relationships as well.

You can't create great situations for others if you haven't created a winning proposition for yourself. Focus on the foundation

You can't create great situations for others if you haven't created a winning proposition for yourself. Focus on the foundation.

Chapter Check

❑ Good relationships with friends, lovers, colleagues, and family members are an important part of a balanced and fulfilling life.

❑ Good relationships depend upon honest communication.

❑ Knowing yourself, your needs, your strengths, and your weaknesses is the place to start building your relationships.

❑ It is important to present your true self from the very start of any relationship.

❑ Build upon an honest foundation of who you truly are.

Chapter

17

The Rewards are Limitless

"The people we are in a relationship with are always a mirror,
reflecting our own beliefs, and simultaneously,
we are mirrors, reflecting their beliefs. So…
relationship is one of the most powerful tools for growth.…
If we look honestly at our relationships,
we can see so much about how we have created them."
—Shakti Gawain

Have you heard the saying, "Behind every man is a great woman"? This is so true, but let's update it a bit. Behind every great person is another great person who believes in him or her. It could be a spouse, a client, a co-worker, a parent, a family member, a friend, or even all of them.

If you have this kind of support, you're lucky. Many times you have to work to find a "supporting cast" for your dreams, goals, and aspirations. We all need someone to help pick us up when we are down and share the excitement and accomplishment of something great. We were programmed to want to share, but we need to make sure we are sharing with people who will help us evolve, not let us stagnate or get weighed down with self-doubt.

Do some people drain you emotionally? If so, discipline yourself to limit your time with them, and if at all possible, stay away from them. I am sure you know exactly the people or person in your life I am talking about. Later on I will get into more detail about how harmful it is to your growth to have negative people around you. On the other hand, are there people you talk to who inspire your thinking, lift you up, and give you a charge? Find a way to keep them close to you as part of your lifelong "supporting cast."

One of the easiest ways to find people who motivate you is to become that person...

Here's a secret. One of the easiest ways to find people who motivate you is to *become* that person—the positive, uplifting, inspiring type of person.

Sometimes the people we love the most may be the ones who we find most challenging to deal with. Your husband, wife, cousin, mother, father, or brother may think you're nuts for trying something different. They don't understand what you understand; they may not think like you think and therefore your changed behavior seems odd to them.

For example, if someone close to you is content working a typical 9 to 5 job and being in an okay relationship, he or she may think it is ridiculous for you to start your own business, move out of town for a new job, or spend the time to put the spark back in your relationship. This person may feel this way because he or she doesn't understand that other options exist. It's okay. It is what it is. If he or she is open to what you're doing, then great. If not, then that's great too. Either way, you can't let them or their words impact you.

Some of the greatest personal success stories in the world today were created and even inspired because the people closest to them thought they were crazy. So realize that you're not alone. And if you have all the support in the world from everyone around you, then thank your lucky stars, because many people had to get started without a supporting cast.

If you have someone pulling you down, then realize there are two things that could happen. Either you are going to bring the person up to your level, or you are going to fall down to the other person's level. Sometimes this may mean putting an end to a relationship that wasn't well grounded in the first place.

Working on your personal and business relationships is a must if you want a Totally Fulfilled life. Whether starting new, taking your current relationship to another level, or possibly ending a relationship that is not healthy for the parties involved, you need to take that part of your life to where it deserves to be. No matter what the past was like, your relationships can be a shining star.

> *...no matter what the past was like, your relationships can be a shining star.*

Communication is Key

As I've said, both of my parents were married four times each. Perhaps that's why I care about relationships so much. I see the struggles both of them had by not having the right people around them and not communicating well with each other. Looking back, I see now that they were constantly trying to change each other or the partners they were with. So I learned what not to do by watching them. Relationships are not about changing the person you are with. They are about knowing and respecting who the other person is and working with each other to achieve goals. The only way you accomplish this is through communication.

Yet as much as I observed my parents and others, I had to make the same mistakes to really understand the power of TRUE communication. Making mistakes is inevitable, but learning from them and not repeating them is a key part of a successful and fulfilled future, especially when it comes to relationships.

I was married for over ten years to a wonderful woman, Melissa, who is still one of my best friends. We seemingly had the perfect relationship. But like with many things in life, we were making small mistakes that were adding up. We focused so much on making everyone and everything around us perfect that we were not in communication enough on the important things. I wanted children right away in our marriage but since we were in our early 20's Melissa wanted to wait. Looking back, that was smart—we were probably too young. Then, by the time Melissa was ready for children I was so engulfed in work and taking on new ventures that I wanted to put it off. I could not imagine finding the time to be the perfect parent I wanted to be. Looking back, you realize there is no perfect time. This led to me working way too many hours and, in our free time, Melissa and I socialized instead of working on a family and our relationship. As my work load grew, our communication got weaker on the important things because when we had time together we just talked about surface level stuff instead of the bigger things that were slowly adding up and pushing us apart. Neither of us liked confrontation. Melissa let things build that were bothering her without me knowing. I made poor decisions because of things bothering me about some of the choices she made, as well. Instead of communicating, sharing, and expressing what was important, we let a relationship that was 90% okay slip away.

Even though Melissa and I are amazing friends and would do anything for each other, it's sad that our marriage failed. It's sad that we had to make mistakes in order to learn from them, but I was taught such valuable lessons about communication or lack thereof. It was tough for me to transform this from a failure into a learned lesson. I know I would not be the person I am today if Melissa had never been in my life. I also know I would have never learned from my mistakes on such a powerful level if we didn't separate. I have evolved so much since we have been apart. I was able to reach inside and find why I made certain decisions and why I did certain things. In retrospect, I know I have become a better person because we parted. I learned the definition and importance of *true* communication in a relationship, and learned what not to do as well as what to do.

You may wonder why Melissa and I are good friends. Why are we both able to enjoy our current lives? I've overcome all the obstacles involved because I used the lessons in this book to build my core. Today, Melissa's family is still like my own and we all continue to keep in touch.

I want you to use everything I share with you in a positive light. I don't focus on why this happened anymore. Whether it was 50% my fault or 100% my fault, I have to focus on how fortunate I was to have amazing people in my life who allowed me to grow, while I know I helped Melissa and her family grow as well. We helped each other financially, emotionally, and physically, and through it all we are still very close. We handled our great times as well as our not-so-great times. Remember, we are not typically judged by the things that are easy, but rather by how we deal with adversity.

Thank you for letting me share that very personal side of my life. I shared that with you so you can avoid similar situations. Like I said at the beginning of this story, I watched my parents make these same mistakes yet I had to deal with the ups and downs of an important relationship myself to learn the impact of communication. There is no reason you need to experience it for yourself if you have faith in my words and life lessons. I urge you to take a look at the relationships in your life and make sure you are representing your thoughts and emotions honestly to a person you may love, a business partner, or maybe a friend or family member. A little communication today can make for a lasting relationship.

> *Mistakes are only a bad thing if you don't learn from them.*

Mistakes are only a bad thing if you don't learn from them.

Today, I am in a relationship with a wonderful woman and our communication is on a totally different level than I knew could exist. Communication and learning from your mistakes can allow you to reach heights that you may never have thought were obtainable.

Proper communication is a key element to relationship success. It's imperative you let people know exactly what you are thinking and not get frustrated if someone does not think exactly like you. If you want to start a new relationship and attract a healthy, nurturing, loving companion, then set the example. Become the person you want to attract and communicate your message. And if you are in a loving relationship that you want to strengthen or take to another level, then communication is still key. Focus on under-

Focus on understanding others, not trying to change them.

standing others, not trying to change them. This goes for your love life, business life, and relationships with friends and family as well.

By laying the groundwork with good communication, you set the stage for a supportive environment for success. If you don't communicate, you'll likely find frustration is inevitable. Here is a statement or phrase I use often to my employees, friends and family: "*Lack of Communication Causes Frustration.*" It's short and to the point. Remember that in your relationship world and you will be enlightened with stronger communication.

Chapter Check

❑ Totally Fulfilled people surround themselves with supportive people—lovers, family, friends, and colleagues.

❑ Assigning blame in a failed relationship prevents you from learning the lessons of the painful experience.

❑ Don't ask *who* is to blame but *how* did it happen and *what* can I do to avoid repeating those same mistakes.

❑ Lack of communication causes frustration.

18

Chapter

Be a Giver

*"I don't know what your destiny will be,
but one thing I know:
the only ones among you
who will be truly happy are those who will have
sought and found how to serve."*
—Albert Schweitzer

Giving is such an important part of relationships. Giving seems like such an easy thing to do. But life can sometimes throw us curve balls that can make it easy for us to feel that we need to receive something before we give something. That's the "what's in it for me" feeling. Life experiences can do this to you, especially if you feel you have been taken advantage of in the past for giving or trusting. We lose sight of the incredible feeling attached to giving unconditionally, especially when it comes to love and relationships.

Most people look at "giving" completely backwards. People think when they start receiving they will give, but it does not work that way. Have you ever heard anyone say, "If I find someone who gives me what I need in a relationship then I will be ready to give back"? Or maybe, "Once I have more time in my life I will give my time to help others"? Or perhaps, "Once I become rich I will give to people in need"? That is not the way it works. You need to give before you receive.

Truths For Living

By William Arthur Ward

The more generous we are,
the more joyous we become.

The more cooperative we are,
the more valuable we become.

The more enthusiastic we are,
the more productive we become.

The more serving we are,
the more prosperous we become.

The more outgoing we are,
the more helpful we become.

The more curious we are,
the more creative we become.

The more patient we are,
the more understanding we become.

If you think you don't have much to give, think again. Recently, I went to a local breakfast place in my neighborhood that I try to frequent every Saturday. It is a comfortable place that has quiet seating outside under shade trees. I use this time to organize the week ahead or just read the paper as I slowly eat my breakfast. Well, this particular morning I was at my favorite place under my shade tree. I was on the phone discussing two real estate deals I was working on, and one was not going well. So I was a bit frustrated and talking fast, writing, thinking, and making other calls to save the deal. I was getting frustrated over a deal that I stood to make about $100,000 on with about a week's worth of work. (Poor me, right?)

As I was talking and writing, I stopped for a minute to eat. When I looked up, I saw a young girl sitting by herself. She didn't have any breakfast in front of her, just her purse and a rolled up apron. She was probably leaving her shift at the restaurant, and was waiting for a ride. She was just sitting with her head down and with really sad eyes. You could tell something was troubling her. I wanted to talk to her and ask if she was okay, to see if she needed money for breakfast, but I also didn't want her to feel uncomfortable about a stranger coming up to her.

I contemplated what to do. Finally, I walked up to her and said, "I'm leaving. Would you like the newspaper I have? I didn't even have a chance to read it." She replied, "Are you serious? Thank you so much. That is so kind." Her face lit up with a smile like I just gave her tickets to Hawaii. I said, "You're welcome and take care." She thanked me again and then said, "This is just what I needed."

As I walked away she started reading the paper and waved again as I drove off. Now, I am not saying I changed this girl's life with a newspaper. But I know she felt cared about, even if it was just for a few moments.

So giving does not require a lot of money or a lot of time. It could be as simple as a smile, or a pat on the back, or asking someone if everything is okay. We have all been blessed with the gift to give, and I promise that you have so much to give others already inside of you. Take advantage of it. Don't expect to get it back in return and watch how things in your life start to change.

It Comes Back Tenfold

As I shared with you earlier, my dad was taken advantage of as a child by an abusive father, so it was hard for him to trust people. Therefore, he found it hard to give of himself. I thank God that in recent years he has been the complete opposite. He can't give enough of himself to others, and it has brought him a happiness and peace he has waited his entire life for.

I saw at a young age the amazing transformational power of giving and how it came back to me even though I was not expecting it. I also saw how my dad's beliefs affected his actions on a regular basis. He told me I was too generous, I gave too much, and I was being a fool in some cases.

This was difficult to overcome, especially as my business ventures started to expand. At a very young age I was already diversifying: car sales, auto body repair, renovating run down apartments, and an Internet company. I started with very little, so every dime I earned came from hard physical work and taking some chances. And this was all going on in my early twenties.

While I was working so hard to diversify and make my life different than that of the people around me, my dad thought I was being foolish with some of the people I trusted. And wouldn't you know it…one of my investments took almost my entire life savings. This was money I had saved for years. The worst part is that it wasn't just a bad investment. Someone I considered a friend flat out conned me.

This person was 35 years my senior. He was someone I felt so strongly about that I asked him to be in my wedding. And with his smiles and hugs and friendly conversations he sucked up all the money I had at the time. I found out later that he had done that to many other people. He started the relationship with me with the intent to defraud me. That experience, combined with a few other "gotchas," could have set me on a course of "I'll give when I get something first" and "I can't trust anyone."

Please don't think I am saying to be foolish with your time or money. Today, if presented with the same deal that sounded great,

I would have given this person the same chance, but I would have taken the time to do a little more homework on his past. And if I didn't like the deal I would have declined with a smile and a handshake.

When this happened, my immediate reaction was that my life was ruined. When I found out the money was gone, I threw my phone on the ground and broke it. I remember saying out loud: "I worked so hard for my money. It's gone and I got nothing from it." I wondered how this could happen to me. Have you ever felt that way? I am sure you have. My limitless beliefs where popping out of my head and mouth faster than I could put a lid on them. Combine that with the "poor me syndrome" and I was the textbook case of what not to do when something goes in the wrong direction. Fortunately, those emotions only lasted an hour before I took a different approach.

At that point, I was young enough and inexperienced enough that the events could have turned me in either direction. I could have set the belief like my dad had at the time, that trusting and giving meant pain, and that not trusting or giving would keep you safe. I can only imagine how my life may have turned out if I chose the supposed "safe" route.

If I had focused on the negative, I never would have had the chance to help so many people. I feel so fortunate that I have come this far and am able to share with you. I know I would not be any-where different than where I was way back then if I didn't overcome the negativity and continue to give.

A year or two later something happened to me that consolidated my thoughts on trust, giving, and looking for the best in people. Let me tell you a quick story that was a big changing point in my life. The person who did it does not even know he affected me in this way.

A Kind Word that Will Last a Lifetime

I was on my way to New York City with a friend who is a bit older than I am. He is a very successful self-made person in the corporate world. At the time, I had come up with an idea that I shared with my friend. He hooked me up with a big company in the city to allow me to present my idea. On the way to Manhattan, which was an hour and a half drive, we were talking about life and business. Needless to say, I was a little nervous but doing all I could to show confidence. My friend had given me a few compliments about how I was progressing in business and doing well for myself. He was much more successful than I was at the time, and he worked just as hard. However, he took a different route than I did. He went to top colleges and graduated with honors.

During the conversation, he asked what I thought my weakest trait was. I said that my weakest trait was I trusted too much—that I tended to give all of me with the hopes of it coming back. I explained that I probably needed to be more aggressive, hold back, and not be so giving or trusting. I started to tell him of the money I had lost because of my weakness.

For the few times you may have been taken advantage of for giving all of you, you have received twenty times more good in your life.

My friend cut me off and replied, "That's funny, Dean. I consider your trust in others as your biggest asset. For the few times you may have been taken advantage of for giving all of you, you have received twenty times more good in your life." (At the time, my friend had a thriving million-dollar business. I was working daily at my auto sales business, fixing cars, remodeling apartments, and writing my Motor Millions program. I was as blue collar as they come, yet he treated me as an equal.) "The reason I am taking you to this meeting, and we have a relationship, is because of your giving heart. People who are afraid to give and afraid to expose themselves will never get what they long for." His final word was to never get cynical no matter how many times you feel taken advantage of—stay who you are.

I still think of his words today. Whenever I get frustrated and want to say "no more," I think of the hundreds of good things that happened to me for trusting rather than the few that hurt me.

Giving is giving and trusting is trusting in all facets of life. I urge you to go out on a limb and give and trust more than ever before in your life: in your personal relationships, in your love life, in doing

People who are afraid to give and afraid to expose themselves will never get what they long for.

business deals, in looking for partners, in sharing your knowledge, in whatever it is. Give all the love you can; give all the compassion you can; give all the secrets you know. Give, give, give, because it will come back to you. It might not come back on your first deal. It might not come back on your first love. But the more you give and the more you have faith in giving, the more it will come back to you in your quest for Total Fulfillment.

I know your past may be telling you otherwise. You may have been burned for loving too much or trusting too much. Maybe someone broke your heart or your bank account. But don't let the past determine your future. Every one of us has been taken advantage of one way or another. In trusting and giving to certain people, I have lost around $2.5 million dollars in my life, and probably lost a few friends because of giving and trusting. On the other side, with a trusting and giving heart I have generated tens of millions of dollars and am fortunate enough to have absolutely amazing people in my life I love dearly. If I had decided fifteen years ago that it would be safer not to trust, my life would never be what it is today, and I would not be here sharing with you right now.

Magic Buttons

Another part of relationships, especially when it comes to business, is something I call "finding the **magic buttons**" in people. If you are negotiating, looking to borrow money, going into a partnership, or buying or selling something, as long as you know someone's "**magic buttons**," then negotiations are easy.

We all have something we're passionate about—something that excites us. If you are trying to purchase something from someone and if you take the time to find out what the other person wants and needs, you will have a better negotiation. Many people think price is the only factor in a negotiation. Price is just one component of the equation. You can create a win/win situation with someone simply by taking the time to listen to what the other person says.

We have two ears and one mouth for a reason. If you are trying to understand someone or a situation by talking, you can't possibly have a listening heart. Remember, it's not what you say; it's how you make the other person feel by truly understanding the circumstances at hand. Allow yourself to grow by listening to what people need to say.

> *"There are two kinds of people in this life.*
> *Those who walk into a room and*
> *say, 'Well, here I am.' And those who walk in and say,*
> *'Ahh, there you are.'*
> *Let us each strive to be an 'Ahh, there you are' person."*
> —Leil Lowndess

Many times in business, people tell me, "There is no way this deal is going to happen." But I love the challenge of turning lemons to lemonade. It's the challenge that makes it great. And the more you practice, the easier it gets. I also think when you love people, the deal is really secondary. I love hearing people's stories, learning about their backgrounds, and understanding their motivations and "magic buttons." If you love people, good deals will ultimately seem to come your way and find you. I have had the supposed hardest people to deal with not only give me a great deal, but also end up being my long-term friends.

As Dale Carnegie said, "When you become genuinely interested in other people, they will be interested in you." And if communicating with new people is not the easiest thing for you at this time, here is a simple tool I learned from a gentleman who specializes in helping people communicate better. It is built on the acronym F.O.R.M. Simply ask people:

- ◆ F = Where are you **from**?

- ◆ O = What is your **occupation**? What kind of work do you do?

- ◆ R = What do you like to do for fun and **recreation** when you're not working?

- ◆ M = What would you do if **money** wasn't an issue for you and your family?

Of course, you can dig a little deeper with each of these questions. You can ask, "What do you like most?" Or, "What would you like to improve in each of these areas?" Those questions will make you stand out in a crowd. With a simple rapport building skill like this one, in a matter of minutes you will likely know the person better than some of their family. By having a genuine love and interest in others, you will be known as a conversationalist—someone who takes the time to care. Always remember, people don't care how much you know; they want to know how much you care. It's all about how you make others feel. Become a lover of people, someone who is genuinely interested in others, and watch the opportunities you attract—and your income—skyrocket.

> *Always remember, people don't care how much you know; they want to know how much you care.*

Why Judge?

When it comes to relationships, so many people are quick to judge the other person—whether it's a family member or business associate—but that is a recipe for a relationship disaster. We are a society that passes judgment before we know the facts, and it is a cause of so much wasted stress and energy. I learned to quit judging, and once I did, my personal life skyrocketed to another level.

Quite honestly, it seemed like a hundred pound weight was lifted off of my shoulders, and it never came back.

My mom is one of the most beautiful women I have ever met, inside and out. She is compassionate, loving, caring, and gives up anything she has to make the people around her feel comfortable. But my mom struggled with insecurity her entire life. She had a learning disability many years ago and did not get the attention she needed to overcome it. She believed she was stupid. That limiting belief stuck with her most of her life, and I know it is the number one reason for her failed relationships.

When my mom and dad divorced, my mom, at the age of 27, had two kids, no job, no financial support, no work skills, and, unfortunately, no self-esteem. She tried to handle all of this while dealing with my dad's rage about the breakup. It was a messy, tough situation, but my mom did what she had to. She cleaned houses, helped out at a beauty salon, took odd jobs, and did everything she could to take care of us. We had to move often; she dated and married the wrong guys, drove junky cars, and when I was about 13, she moved out of state with her husband at the time.

As I think back, even though I remember worrying about her, she did not complain, and she always showed us love unconditionally. From the outside, she may not have looked like the best mom. If I hadn't known her circumstances, I probably would have believed that exterior image, too, when I was growing up. But I know how much adversity she had to deal with, and in fact, my mom was the opposite of what she appeared to be. She was a superwoman, battling constantly for her children, and doing the best she could with the hand she was dealt.

Looking back, I would not change one thing about my childhood or my mom because they allowed me to become the person I am today. I know that watching my mom struggle for most of my young life was the main reason I wanted more out of my life. I wanted her to have a better life, too, not to struggle, and to be able to smile and mean it. Without knowing it, she gave me so many gifts—gifts that will last a lifetime.

To this day, my mom will get frustrated on occasion and say "I'm so stupid." I tell her that she is the most amazing person in the world. We can't all be perfect in every area of life. A great pitcher on a baseball team may stink at batting, and in fact, most do. A professional racecar driver like Jeff Gordon, as good as he may be, would get destroyed if he played a one-on-one basketball game against Michael Jordan and vice versa.

So Mom has trouble spelling and has other minor learning disabilities. But as a mother who was handed a pile of adversity, she was the absolute best she could be. And can anyone ask for more than that? Not the way I see it. When it comes to love, caring, and giving all of herself to other people, she is the Tiger Woods of mothers, the best at what she does.

I tell you this story because we never really know what people are going through or what they have gone through in their life. Looking from the outside, we can never know what someone else's obstacles may be, and they may not know ours.

We shouldn't assume and judge, but we do, all the time.

Know in your heart that the world will be a better place and your relationships will be stronger if you don't judge too harshly, and if you don't form opinions about people or circumstances without the facts. We must learn to *accept* others, sometimes without an explanation and always without judgment.

There are thousands of stories like my mother's, everywhere, every day. Try to be aware of them and the lessons they can teach you.

I was recently reminded yet again not to judge. I am 100% guilty of being on my cell phone way too much. I have a lot of different things going on in my life, and time is very important. So, if I am driving, I optimize my time by making necessary phone calls. And I know that trying to dial and answer phone calls while driving is not the smartest thing to do, because it is definitely distracting. Luckily, I have never done anything that caused an accident or even came close. But I see why some states ban cell phone use in cars, and I now have a voice-activated system.

One day, my mom called my cell phone while I was driving. She said that I might want to come to Virginia to see my grandmother because she wasn't doing well, and my mom feared she might not live long. Because I lived in Phoenix, I didn't get to see my grandmother as much as I would have liked, so it was hard news. I wanted to get to Virginia right away.

I have to admit I was a bit distracted. I went to pull over, and I accidentally cut another driver off in traffic. Well, the guy I cut off flipped me off, yelling out his window, "Hey, a****e, why don't you get off your cell phone and learn how to drive?!"

As he sped away, I could see that he was angry and waving his hands. He judged me instantly without considering why I might have needed to pull over quickly. In his eyes, I was just a guy in a Mercedes on the cell phone, and automatically he judged me, got angry, and wasted his energy being furious with me.

That man could have never known my circumstances; he just judged. If he had had the chance to listen to my phone conversation, would he have reacted differently? What if he knew in a second what kind of person I was, and that I didn't mean any harm to him at all? No doubt he would have acted with more compassion.

> *Why waste even one second of energy on something negative, something that only hurts you?*

Why, then, wouldn't it make sense to just not judge anyone when you don't know the facts? Why waste even one second of energy on something negative, something that only hurts you?

There are always an infinite number of reasons why someone may cut you off or drive poorly, and none of them have anything to do with you. What if the driver is ill? What if he or she is rushing to the hospital for an emergency? What he or she just lost a job and is distracted? What if the driver has a disability?

What if, for the rest of your life, every time a person cut you off in traffic, no matter how it looked, you said to yourself, or even to God, "I hope everything is okay with that person." Over your lifetime, imagine how much wasted energy that simple action would save you for more positive thoughts!

How much time and energy have you wasted in *your* life feeling angry, vengeful, hurt, or upset over something that really didn't matter? Have you taken someone's words or actions personally, when they really weren't about you at all? How many judgments have you made without knowing all of the facts?

Imagine how much extra energy you would have for positive thoughts and your more fulfilled life if you stopped doing that today!

How much time and energy have you wasted in your life feeling angry, vengeful, hurt, or upset over something that really didn't matter?

You could approach all circumstances and relationships in your life this same way.

◆ When a friend, a family member, or a loved one does something that you think is wrong or that offends you, take a moment and ask yourself if you really know why he or she did it, or if you just *assume* you know why. Give the people you love or *anyone* the benefit of the doubt that they are not deliberately trying to hurt you.

◆ When someone makes bad decisions, instead of judging them for their choices, feel sympathy for them and wish them good thoughts because they don't have the skills you possess to change your beliefs and change your life.

I know the power of living this way, without assumptions and judgment, because when I am around someone who makes mean remarks about people or gets upset easily by others, I simply share the message I have shared with you, and instantly people think differently. Once you see how good it feels to live your life this way, share it with others.

Chapter Check

❑ Being generous doesn't always mean giving people money or gifts.

❑ Even the smallest kind gesture can have a ripple effect in the world.

❑ Even if one person takes advantage of your generous nature, don't stop giving.

❑ Giving your trust to others will always pay dividends in the long run.

❑ To develop successful relationships, you need to find out what other people's Magic Buttons are—what they are passionate about, what motivates, excites them, etc.

❑ If you have trouble with getting to know people, you can always rely on F.O.R.M.: From, Occupation, Recreation, Money.

❑ Sometimes the greatest gift you can give someone is the benefit of the doubt.

Chapter 19

Beware of Other People's Opinions

"Just don't give up trying to do what you really want to do.
Where there is love and inspiration,
I don't think you can go wrong"
—Ella Fitzgerald

I just finished sharing with you that a fulfilled person gives people the benefit of the doubt and always looks for the best in others. Now it may seem like a contradiction but I am going to share with you a key factor in your journey towards a fulfilled life. It's important to understand the difference between giving someone the benefit of the doubt and letting other people's opinions of you or your ideas influence you in a negative way.

If you asked 20 people you know why they failed in a certain area of life, I would bet that a majority of them would give the name of a person that held them back or did not support them. This is where, without experience, other people's perceptions or limited ideas can become your reality if you are not trained to acknowledge their influence and prevent them from doing harm.

In this chapter it is my goal to have you maintain a positive outlook about people while at the same time being able to immediately identify if someone is holding you back from a life more fulfilled. This does not mean these are people are deliberately trying to hurt you, but their actions can negatively impact your life.

> *No one can make you feel inferior or tell you your ideas or vision is wrong unless you allow them that power.*

I have seen many people fail because they let other people steal their dreams and instill a sense of negativity. Remember this—no matter how well-intentioned someone is, or what his or her relationship is with you, if you do what others tell you, you will likely have what they have. If they don't have what you want in life, then why are they qualified to guide you or make you feel a certain way? No one can make you feel inferior or tell you your ideas or vision is wrong unless you allow them that power.

Many times you can tell the quality of a person by the advice he or she gives. Is he or she the type of person who points out the faults, the problems, the challenges, the downfalls, the risks, and the negative? Remember, anyone can find weeds in the garden.

On the other hand, is he or she constructive? Does the person find the solutions with an alternative? Does he or she offer supporting ideas? Does the person applaud your goals and dreams with support?

You want advice from someone who says, "Let me tell you why it didn't work for me and how it could possibly work for you," not someone who says, "It didn't work out for me, so don't even try to do it." That's an important difference, wouldn't you agree?

It's all in the language. Unsuccessful people are trained to find what's wrong. They say, "Here's why it won't work." Successful people, on the other hand, go beyond this average way of thinking and say, "Here's what's wrong, and here's the solution and alternative to make it better. Here's why it won't work, and here are the other possibilities to get the results you're looking for."

Consider the Source

Let me give you an example. You could get advice from someone who has never experienced what you're trying to achieve. If you have a loved one or family member who has never done anything except work a 9-5 job (and who is probably afraid to take chances in life), they're likely to have a limited and structured way of thinking. This person's optimal level of success may be working for a big company and retiring at age sixty-five. Remember, perception is reality.

Is that the kind of person you want to get advice from for starting your own business? Of course not. The person is going to tell you you're nuts and that you need to get a job and work more hours.

I had a certain family member who always told me I was crazy when I used to say I was going to be self-employed when I got older, make a ton of money, and make a difference in the world. He would ask me how, and I would say that I wasn't sure but that I was going to do it. I was about ten years old the first time I said that.

Each time he told me I was crazy, I used to get upset. He would say, "Dean, you're always reaching for the stars. Sometimes you need to just realize what your limits are and be happy with what you have." I used his jabs to motivate me.

Now don't get me wrong, I do enjoy what I have, but I love striving and accomplishing more. While he's sitting on the couch, I'm changing my life and the lives of others.

In life, there are those who make things happen, those who watch what happens, and those who ask, "What happened?" Make a commitment to stand out from the crowd and go for it no matter what people say. This does not mean you have to judge anyone in a negative way. In fact, in my life it has become the complete opposite. When someone expresses to me their limited belief or criticizes me for something I want to accomplish, I've trained myself to instantly feel bad for them because of their small thinking. If time allows, I try to show them a different way of thinking and if they don't accept, then they are the ones who will struggle, always wondering what it is like to live life on another level.

Find someone who is climbing, changing lives, and making things happen, and then grab a hold of that person.

Alternatively, you might consider getting advice or learning from someone who is successful—someone who lives the life you would like to live or specializes in an area in which you want to be fulfilled. Realize that I speak in terms of success differently than most. Success isn't just dollars and cents. It's the whole package. If you're not climbing, you're sliding. Find someone who is climbing, changing lives, and making things happen, and then grab a hold of that person.

A perfect example of this is that recently I have had the desire to explore and expand my relationship with God. I have always been a Christian yet being so busy in my adult life I never took the time to get to know God beyond what I learned from going to Catholic school until the 5th grade. Like we discussed in an earlier chapter, I put the word out there that these were my thoughts. I told family and friends and asked advice from people who already had an empowering relationship with God. In a meeting with a business associate and also good friend I told him of my desire to expand that part of my life. I knew it was my time to search and find fulfillment in this area of my life. Damon, my associate, shared with me a different side of God's words that I was not used to hearing. Or maybe I was not listening until now. We had a great conversation and he felt great sharing his passion. A few weeks later Damon called me and asked if I would fly to Jacksonville, Florida, to meet a family friend named Joel Osteen. I had seen Joel on TV before and thought he was a great speaker. I also knew he had a book out called *Your Best Life Now* that was not only a best seller but was loved by everyone I knew who read it. So I said "what the heck", kept an open mind, and booked a flight to Jacksonville to hear Joel live and then meet him after his service.

I was not sure what to expect but I knew if I was going to reach out and try to expand my relationship with God, Joel Osteen seemed like the guy who could help me get there. You have to understand that I grew up Catholic, which had some very tough guidelines for what was right and wrong. Also when I was a kid I was under the misguided belief that TV evangelists were in it for just the money. So I had to throw those limiting beliefs in the garbage and go see Joel with an open mind and an open heart.

I was blown away with what Joel was sharing with people. He allowed people to see the connection between success in your life and God in such a simple manner. He didn't cram God down your throat like many others I had seen on TV through the years. I liked the fact of feeling the love of God rather than the fear of going to hell for not being perfect. I personally felt empowered on another level. While preaching, Joel seemed kind and truly caring, attributes that I hoped were sincere. After the service I met Joel, his wife Victoria, his mom, and his brother. Every single one of them lives the life they teach, preach, and try to share with others. The fact was that Joel not only talks the talk, he walks the walk. I've since flown to his Lakewood church in Houston simply to participate in another service and meet him once again; his message and caring stayed consistent. If I was going to take advice or find a mentor to expand my relationship with God, then Joel would be my guy.

I don't think I will ever be a preacher or a perfect Christian and I will never push God on anyone who does not want to learn what I have experienced. But I have found a new relationship with God that I enjoy and it is because I learned from and was inspired by someone who was doing it in a big, important way, in a way that I wanted to model. I have had friends and even family members make a joke about the fact that I wanted to explore this area of my life. I chose to let their words bounce off me and not affect the desire I had to learn and grow spiritually.

If you have a desire to explore your spirituality or your faith then I say go for it and don't let friends, family, or past experiences deter your exploration. If you would like to see what I felt when I saw Joel or see what he is about you can go to my web site www.totallyfulfilled.com and clink on the link to his web site.

I believe you can learn from just about anybody— even if it's what not to do.

It does not matter what area or areas of your life you want to make expand or improve. You can find a lot of great coaches and mentors in the world today. In fact, I believe you can learn from just about anybody—even if it's what not to do. You simply have to get control of you, your thoughts, and who you allow to influence you.

If you are having relationship problems, you may not want to take advice from your single friends who may be lonely. Likewise, you wouldn't want to take advice from a family member who feels cheated in a relationship.

My point is simple. Take advice that fuels you. Take advice from people who've been there and done it and continue to do it. Don't let the wrong people steal your dreams.

No One Can Steal Your Dreams Without Your Permission

You may have people in your life who hold you back from reaching the level of success, happiness, and fulfillment you can achieve, and you don't even realize it. I don't know where I heard the phrase "dream stealer," but I said it at a seminar once and the entire audience rumbled. Many said they had several in their life.

I want you to identify that someone in your life who, when you reveal the changes you want to make, discourages you and holds you back. The worst part is that the person in your life who may be discouraging you or influencing you in a negative way is

You Can Do It

by Jerry Aragon, Ph. D. (Phunny humor Doctor)
www.humordoctormd.homestead.com/

Peer pressure is not just for teenagers!
The ugly face of peer pressure will follow us all to the grave,
by those who would have us go
in a different direction with our lives!

So, decide what you want in life,
and don't let anyone distract you
from reaching your goals and your dreams!

not necessarily against you or a bad person; rather, he or she just doesn't understand your passion and may be afraid of change.

The toughest dream stealers are your family. Beside yourself, they can be your worst critics. They think they're protecting you. Sometimes they're jealous because they wanted to be where you want to go and either they didn't try, or they tried and failed. Either way, they love to keep you safe and protected. Safe and protected to them can be a whole different definition from where you are headed.

Other dream stealers come in the form of "experts." As you may know, years ago I created a program called Motor Millions. My Motor Millions program taught people how to make money with automobiles. Cars were the launching pad for my success at an early age. My dad had been in the car business when I was in high school so I knew the profit that could be made. In fact I decided not to go to college so I could work with my dad in his car business. Yet a few years out of high school my dad hit a few obstacles all at once and closed down his auto sales business. When left with no money, no college degree, and no job I became very inventive about how to make money in car sales, starting with no money. In fact, I started matching buyers and sellers, making a profit in the middle, then started using those profits to buy and sell my own cars. The following year I bought the building my father had lost and just a year later did over $500,000 in sales.

When I started making money with cars, I had friends and family coming out of the woodwork who needed to borrow money. I thought to myself, "If I just lend them money, they're going to be back for more." So I looked at the problem of people needing money and figured out a way for them to make money with cars the same way I was doing it. I started teaching friends and family my simple principles. Some of the ideas worked. Some didn't. I kept refining the ideas until I came up with an ultimate system for all types of people—even those with no experience—to profit from used cars. It felt great, and I loved helping them make money. But I didn't stop there. Their success inspired me to go further. I felt that if I could help a few, I could help thousands of people.

I had seen infomercials on TV where people shared their success in a step-by-step course, and I said, "I can do that." So I studied their shows and came up with an idea to help people all over the country make money like I did. What could be more gratifying than that? I could have the chance to make money while I helped other people make money. You can only imagine how many "You're crazy," "You're nuts," and "That will never work" statements I heard. But I went with my gut.

So I would get up early in the morning before I went to work with my auto sales company and write the books and manuals on how people could do what I did. When I was done with the manuals and the videos to teach people, I figured it was time to do a TV show. I didn't know what I was going to do, or even how I would do it. I was passionate about my goal and figured it out along the way. I wrote my script, hired a producer, and filmed the first show on the front yard of my house.

Understand that this was scary for me to do back then. I took a big risk. I was using my credit cards and borrowed money to finance everything. I was doing whatever I could to make this thing happen. It was scary and exciting at the same time. I got through it by focusing on the end result: success.

Next, it was time to get it on TV, and I was unsure of what to do. So I looked through the phone book for people who would buy TV time. I was clueless getting started, but I was doing it. Then I had a brilliant idea (or so I thought) and hired a gentleman who was an expert in this field. He had been responsible for some of the top infomercials on TV. He had experience and seemed to believe in my program. Before I knew it, we had a contract, and I agreed to give him a full five percent of all the gross sales. I was clueless. In that business, you can do big dollar amounts in sales because you are nationwide, but you operate on very minimal profit margins. So, in essence, I gave him a huge share of the company—probably more than half. But it was okay, because I was getting his advice, his expertise, and having him point me in the right direction.

I figured that he was an expert and that I needed him. I can either pay with the mistakes I'll make, or I can pay for him to save me time and money. It seemed to make sense at the time.

We finalized the details, and I was off to work. I filmed, edited, wrote the script, and created the program concept from A to Z. Then we launched an initial test on TV. I was excited! All the hard work seemed so close to paying off. I was smiling ear to ear for a week… until that phone call.

This gentleman called and said, "Dean, your show's not going to work." I was in shock and replied, "What are you talking about? We've come this far, and the numbers are looking pretty good from what I can see." He said, "I reanalyzed the entire concept, and my guess is that people are not excited about making money with cars."

I tried to explain to him that it wasn't just about cars. It was a tool to give people a simple way to make money. They could simply match buyers and sellers together and make money like I had done. I asked if we could possibly tweak the show. He said, "Dean, unfortunately, it's over."

I hung up the phone, shocked and sad. Looking back, I realize it was another one of those defining moments in my life. It sure didn't feel too defining at the time. It just stunk. The thoughts immediately popped in my head. Was it thousands of dollars and hundreds of hours wasted? Was I to believe that this was a total failure? Should I have ever tried such an unfamiliar task? I had always worked hard, and after losing all my money to a scam in my very early twenties, now I had used all my saved money once again, plus money borrowed on credit cards and from friends.

> *I realized that successful people all have one thing in common: they focus on solutions and don't give up.*

But my experiences were adding up by this time in my life. I reflected back on my past failures and accomplishments. I looked at how most successful people hit walls. I realized that successful people all have one thing in common: they focus on solutions and don't give up. So that's what I did. I used everything I am sharing with you in this book and snapped myself out of any negativity and was immediately rejuvenated with the focus I could do this on my own.

The next day I decided that no one was going to steal my dreams unless I gave them permission. I said out loud: "This is who I am as a person! I preach success to other people! I'm not going to let this stop me. I am going to make my idea work, and if it doesn't, then I know I gave it everything I had."

The so-called expert opted out of his contract, convinced the project was a loser. So I went at it alone, employing trial and error as my tutors. It was definitely not easy, but it worked out. I was able to help people all over the country make money like I did, while at the same time the company did tens of millions of dollars in sales.

Even in the heat of adversity, I realized that what appeared to be the end was really the beginning. My experience has taught me that **all adversity is a new door of opportunity.** This way of thinking was starting to really come to life because it was working. It went from theory to reality.

Even if Motor Millions had been a total failure, I still would have received the knowledge and experience from it that would have allowed me to go to another level in life. If that never happened, or if I gave up because of what another person said, then I am sure I would not be writing this book for you today.

This story is just one of so many in my life that illustrates how focusing on a solution ends with amazing results and life experiences. You need to play this game of life with your rules, not anyone else's. No matter what it is—your love life, your relationships with friends and family, your health, or your emotions—don't let an unqualified "dream stealer" take away your juice for more out of life.

In this chapter it may seem that I took you in circles. I shared with you how important it is to not let unqualified people deter you from reaching your personal goals. I told you how empowering it can be to have a mentor or follow the lead of someone who is living life as you would like to live it.

Ultimately you need to pick and choose the advice and the people who inspire you, drive you, and encourage you to follow your dreams. I shared with you so many variables because I want you to have the power to immediately identify the people who will lift you up and the others that unknowingly or knowingly may bring you down and halt your growth. When in your heart, you know that you have to try something, I say go for it. In my experience it is better to try and fail and learn a lesson than to not try at all.

In my experience it is better to try and fail and learn a lesson than to not try at all.

Chapter Check

❑ Surround yourself with positive people who respect your ideas.

❑ Go with your gut—don't let other people's opinions derail your plans.

❑ Define and play by the rules of your own life.

❑ Stay true to your dreams.

❑ Your true effort is always rewarding: take a positive lesson from every attempt, even if you don't succeed.

Chapter 20

Be a Person of Your Word

"The best index to a person's character is
a) how he treats people who can't do him any good and
b) how he treats people who can't fight back."
—Abigail Van Buren

Sometimes the toughest person to be true to is yourself. Being true, honest, and a person of your word will not only allow people around you to change, but it will also give you an inner sense of peace. This is an essential key to a long-term life of fulfillment.

Success is not always convenient, and when things get tough, we all have the tendency to take the easy route, even if it compromises your word or who you are. I know I have been tempted many times by this common factor when trying to go to another level in life. And in most cases, I took the high road. But in some cases, I did not. I compromised who I was or my word to avoid

> *There is only one way to total long-term fulfillment, and that is to be a person of your word, even when it's not convenient.*

losing something, and each time I did, I regretted it. Even if money or temporary happiness came from it, I felt unfulfilled because I was untrue to myself.

There is only one way to total long-term fulfillment, and that is to be a person of your word, even when it's not convenient. It's easy to be a person of your word when things are good, but you will evolve to another level of life if you can do the same when times are tough.

Through Thick and Thin

I want to share a story about what happened to my company, Motor Millions. Earlier, I told you of the amazing feelings I had and the great accomplishment I achieved by starting this company from nothing and turning it into a multi-million dollar company, even through the adversity that I faced. Yet there was a not-so-amazing time in the history of that company.

Several years into the business, I had accomplished many of the things I wanted to when I started that company. So when I was approached to sell the company and still receive a weekly royalty, I decided I would go for it and work on other ventures I had on my "to do" list. It seemed like a perfect solution towards my evolution.

Unfortunately, even though the purchasing company had a lot of experience in this industry, they didn't care about my customers the same way I did. Their short-term vision and greed quickly turned the company in the wrong direction—putting it on the brinks of bankruptcy in a very short period of time.

Fortunately, the contract was structured so that if certain guidelines were violated, I had the right to take the company back. After six months of this group haphazardly running my company, I had no choice but to file the proper motions with the courts and

take the company back. My name and my reputation were attached to that program.

When I took the company back, I was in shock at what had happened in a fairly short amount of time. This group and the way they handled the business put the company in a tremendous amount of debt. In fact, it ended up costing me over $1 million dollars, much of that in the form of refunds owed to people. Let me tell you how important it is to make sure refunds are always paid and why what they did was so bad.

I would like to start by saying this. If you sent 100 people to your favorite restaurant, it would be fair to guess that maybe 15 of them would not like it no matter what. Maybe it was not their type of food, maybe it was a busy night and they did not like the service, or maybe it just didn't have the right feel for them. Well the same goes in my business. The principles in my Motor Millions kit allowed me to make a fortune starting with nothing. It also allowed people from all over the country who got my kit to make a ton of money as well. But for roughly 15% or so of the people who got my program, it just wasn't for them. Maybe they didn't like the system once they got it, maybe it seemed like too much work, maybe we had a bad day and they felt they did not get proper service when they called. Whatever it was, they wanted to return what they purchased. So for example, if you're doing $200,000 a week in sales and you have a 15% refund rate of people saying it was not for them, then that's an average of $30,000 a week in refunds. Well this new company decided not to pay refunds right away and use that extra money to expand the company. It snowballed and they ended up in the 6-month period paying very few refunds to customers who requested their money back. So you can see how fast that debt can build. And what was even worse is that no one knew I had sold the company. People saw me on TV, they ordered a program I created and they heard me announce the 30-day money back guarantee. If they wanted a refund, they wanted it from me.

I had now taken back a company in huge debt, my name was being compromised—which drove me crazy—customers were getting more and more upset because their refunds were not paid on time, and I had some important decisions to make. My attorney and accountant recommended I file Chapter 11 and walk away from the business. From a business standpoint, I legally had every right to file bankruptcy, and not worry about the debt and refunds. Yet I had a knot in my stomach when I even thought of taking that road. So I followed my own advice and decided to do my best to pay off the debt and keep the company open. The moment I made that decision, the knot in my stomach went away. I came up with a strategic game plan to pay back the creditors and the unpaid refunds that built up while I was not there. Many people who requested refunds where delayed in getting their payment but they were *not denied* and that was what allowed me to stay positive and hold my head high through this tough situation. Did I handle it perfectly? Probably not, but I was true to myself and handled it the best way I knew how.

> *...take responsibility, focus on a solution, and fight your hardest for an outcome that allows you to be true to yourself.*

When things like this happen in life, it is very hard not to fall into the "Why me?" syndrome. But you can be the victim, or you can take responsibility, focus on a solution, and fight your hardest for an outcome that allows you to be true to yourself. It would have been easy to blame the company I sold to, but what good would that have done? Plus, I'm an adult, and I made the decision to sell so I could further my career, and now I had to take responsibility to repair what was not right.

When I realized how messed up things had gotten, I took Motor Millions off the air. Here was the dilemma though: Taking the program off the air meant I stopped generating revenues yet still had ongoing bills and a huge amount of past debt. It was a very tough situation.

I decided I would work hard in other areas to make the money I was losing with Motor Millions and pay back the debt and refunds. I ended up putting up to $20,000 a week into Motor Millions from money I was generating from my other businesses. This went on for well over a year. In fact, to this day I still have a customer service staff that I pay from other income sources to make sure any old customers with questions, or possible old refund requests, are handled properly. It was a very costly lesson, but one I am glad I learned.

How would you feel if people looked at you and knew that your word or your handshake or your verbal commitment was as strong as any contract? It would make you feel proud of yourself, I can assure you of that. Can you be perfect in every situation all the time? Of course not. But if you made the conscious decision today to commit to something and do your best, then your life will flow towards prosperity on so many levels.

Remember that if everything in life was taken away from you, and you had to start over with nothing, your word may be one of the only things you have left. So cherish this amazing gift you have to be a person of your word. I challenge you to do the right thing, and be a good person even when it isn't convenient. It will reward you in ways you never thought possible.

Relationships in all areas of your life, even with yourself, can open the door to massive success on all levels.

Chapter Check

❏ Your self-respect is more valuable than money.

❏ Be a person of your word and others will respect you.

❏ Do the right thing because it is the right thing to do.

❏ You will be rewarded in the long run for being a person of your word.

Section Summary

❑ Totally Fulfilled people surround themselves with supportive *people*—lovers, family, friends, colleagues.

❑ Good *relationships* with lovers, family, friends, and colleagues are an important part of a balanced and fulfilling life.

❑ Good relationships depend upon honest communication.

❑ Knowing yourself, your needs, your strengths, and your weaknesses is the place to start building your relationships.

❑ It is important to present your true self from the very start of any relationship.

❑ Build upon an honest foundation of who you truly are.

❑ Assigning blame in a failed relationship prevents you from learning the lessons of the painful experience.

❑ Don't ask *who* is to blame but *how* did it happen and *what* can I do to avoid repeating those same mistakes.

❑ Lack of communication causes frustration.

❑ Being generous doesn't always mean giving people money or gifts.

❑ Even the smallest kind gesture can have a ripple effect in the world.

❑ Even if one person takes advantage of your generous nature, don't stop giving.

❑ Giving your trust to others will always pay dividends in the long run.

❑ To develop successful relationships, you need to find out what other people's Magic Buttons are—what they are passionate about, what motivates, excites them, etc.

❑ If you have trouble getting to know people, you can always rely on F.O.R.M. From, Occupation, Recreation, Money.

❑ Sometimes the greatest gift you can give someone is the benefit of the doubt.

❑ Surround yourself with positive people who respect your ideas.

❑ Go with your gut—don't let other people's opinions derail your plans.

❑ Define and play by the rules of your own life.

❑ Stay true to your dreams.

❑ Your self-respect is more valuable than money.

❑ Be a person of your word and others will respect you.

❑ Do the right thing because it is the right thing to do.

❑ You will be rewarded in the long run for being a person of your word.

Part 5

Chapter 21

Choose to Be Fulfilled

"Your own words are the bricks and mortar
of the dreams you want to realize.
Your words are the greatest power you have.
The words you choose and their use establish the
life you experience."
—Sonia Croquette

We have been building your foundation for success to get to this point. This section brings it all together as you focus on hitting the "bulls-eye" to living a life Totally Fulfilled. Although this section resembles goal setting, please don't set it aside as just another goal setting exercise. I'm willing to bet that my views on traditional goal setting will surprise you.

In the past, goal setting meant something different to me than what it means now. For years I achieved major accomplishments without ever writing down a goal. Yes, I consciously knew what I wanted to accomplish, but I never took the time to actually put a lot of thought into it and write it down.

As crazy as it sounds, I view accomplishments and goals like digging a ditch. If a person needed a ditch dug, he or she could do it one of two ways. Option one is to analyze the ditch, think how long it might take to dig it, and make it a four day goal to get it done. Option two, and the option I always choose, is to grab a shovel, start digging, and never lift my head up until the ditch is done. That "Do It" attitude seems to work very well for me. I have accomplished more than I ever imagined, so I figure why change it?

As I matured, I realized I sometimes moved too fast and went after things that were not really a strong goal. Although my "ready, fire," approach did work for me, I have to admit that I'd be further ahead if I would have taken the "ready, **aim**, fire approach," backed with a compelling reason and massive action.

A Reason Approach to Goal Setting

One of the main reasons I never set goals was because I thought the words "Goal Setting" had a negative association attached to them. The phrase seemed overused, and it was a task non-doers undertook to make it seem like they were taking action. All the people I had met who overused the phrase seemed to do more reading and attending seminars about success than actually going after what they wanted. Today, the phrase "Goal Setting" still doesn't mean anything to me if there is no substance or reason behind the goal. In fact, I would rather call it "Dreams about to become a reality."

We talked earlier about how events and people can help set limiting beliefs inside of you that can last a lifetime if you don't flush them out and fix them. A variety of things have contributed to me being against traditional goal setting. I didn't like it when people would tell me what they were going to do and then never follow through. I thought it was a sign of weakness. So I always tried to accomplish something and let the act speak for itself.

One specific event helped reinforce this feeling. When I was running my collision/auto sales business, I had a regular client who always came in carrying a briefcase. One day when he popped it open on my desk, I saw the two things he carried in this fairly large briefcase: 1) a check for me, and 2) a sheet of paper that had his "Goals" on it.

He saw me look at the paper and offered to explain what it was. He explained that these were his goals for the next year. And boy, did he have some doozies on the list: a new house, fancy cars, his own business, an airplane, limo…you name it. He was a great guy, and he sat and talked with me about all he the things he was going to do in the next year.

Most of the goals were financial, and he never once spoke of the reason why he wanted all these things. He just seemed to want them because they sounded good, and he definitely did not offer a plan of how he was going to get them.

A year later, he came back for some car repair services. Within minutes, he was talking about all the things he had going on, and all the goals he had set for the New Year. However, he still did not tell me the reason why he wanted all these things. As I listened, I realized he had not achieved a single goal from the previous list.

His goals were just empty wishes with no foundation to build upon. That instance made me see goals as something for dreamers not doers. Why write down things you want or things you want to do if you don't have the right core to build from and actually make them happen, or a strong reason and plan how to get them? I determined at that point that "Goal Lists" were for dreamers, and I was a doer.

Since then, I have learned amazing techniques to turn your dreams and goals into reality. I still believe that just writing down a goal and sticking it on your refrigerator is worth nothing. But goals constructed with a reason for setting them (and with the knowledge that you have learned in this book that anything is possible) is a must towards a Totally Fulfilled life. "Goal Setting", done right, can be one of the most powerful tools for your future success.

If you have thoughts about setting goals, good or bad, I ask you to be open to what I'm about to tell you. It may be non-conventional, but it works. My experience proves it takes so much more than just writing down a goal and hoping it will magically come to life. Any goal needs roots to grow. It needs a purpose. You can't base a goal on past experiences. Rather, you must focus on where you want to go. In this state of mind, you refuse to lose. Obstacles and excuses are not an option as you are committed and prepared to get more out of life. You deserve it; we all do.

My goal is to put you in the mindset of reaching deeper inside of yourself than ever before. I want to challenge you to set goals that are what you really want. I am going to take you through a fun process in preparation for setting goals that will ultimately change your life forever. I have unlocked simple secrets to make your goals, "dreams about to become a reality." If you are still with me, that means you want to make a difference.

Before we get to the fun process of setting the actual goals, you still need a few key factors that will enable your goals to stick for a lifetime.

Be a Doer

By Changing Your Thinking

Author Unknown

*By Changing Your Thinking,
You change your beliefs;*

*When you change your beliefs,
You change your expectations;*

When you change your expectations,
You change your attitude;

When you change your attitude,
You change your behavior;

When you change your behavior,
You change your performance;

When you change your performance;
You Change Your Life!

While most people are out talking, thinking, reading, or researching an idea, successful people are out there doing things and making things happen. As I said earlier, it's not so much about the knowledge; it's actually going out and applying what you know. You'll learn more in a few hours doing than in all the days and months of research and contemplation. You can have all the knowledge in the world, but if you don't apply it, then it's useless.

I see so many people get caught up in thinking they need to know every little detail about something before they take action. In many cases this ends up being a missed opportunity. How many times in life have you come up with an idea or an invention or a business concept and you did not take action? Maybe you analyzed and talked the idea to death. And then several years later you see your idea making someone else a fortune. How about when you are thinking of talking to someone you are interested in, but you put it off? And then you find out he or she is with someone else. It can break your heart and cause you to have tremendous regret. It's always better to try and fail than to never try at all.

I know we grow up hearing contradicting catch phrases, such as "Look before you leap" and "He who hesitates is lost." It's no wonder we are confused. Please know I am not telling you to be careless and leap without doing any research. But if you want more out of life you need to separate yourself from people who just talk about making changes and become the person who does it!

You Only Have To Be Right Once

I want to challenge you to a new way of thinking. It may be hard in the beginning, because I'm going against what you've been trained to do. In school, you learned that in order to be a good student you had to score 100%. However, I've learned that you don't have to be an "A" student to be successful.

If you are right just 51% of the time playing stocks, you'll likely be a very rich person. If you were a baseball player and got a hit 51% of the time, you would be the best the world has ever seen. Yet in school, if you got 51% of the questions correct, you would be graded as a failure.

When resistance appears doers continue and talkers stop.

In your business, if you figure out all the wrong ways to do something and ultimately find the one "best" way to do it, you could develop incredible wealth, but you may have been wrong 90% of the time to find that winning combination. It just takes one "right" answer to crack the code to massive success. Realize that just about anything great has been met with resistance. When resistance appears doers continue and talkers stop. We all know that Thomas Edison invented the light bulb. But did you know that his first 2,000 + attempts at creating the light bulb were a failure? After he had finally figured it out and created the light bulb, someone asked him, "Mr. Edison, what about the 2,000 failures?" He responded: "I didn't fail 2,000 times. I found 2,000 ways to NOT create the light bulb." A different way of thinking and certainly more positive.

The more time you spend doing rather than talking, the quicker you will get the wrong answers out of the way and start finding the solutions. When that happens, you will be able to spend more time "Doing" it right—and that is likely your motive.

Being a doer goes hand-in-hand with the phrase: "If you are not part of the solution then you are part of the problem." I grew up in a small town where everyone knew each other's business. Even in small towns politics plays a part, and everybody had their opinions on how the town should evolve, yet most people just spewed lots of negative words, offered coffee house solutions, and had no desire to really help. So at a young age I decided that instead of just talking about helping our small town, I was going to do something.

Within a few years I ended up being the youngest member of the town planning board. I helped start and became the co-chairman of the town's first Economic Development Committee. I played an active role in an organization that held fundraisers that donated their funds to help local people in need. I also became the secretary of a local governmental committee in our area. Yes, my life was busy, but I felt that if I was going to talk about anything wrong with the town then I had an obligation to be a part of the solution.

So get out there and make it happen. Don't be someone who just talks about making a change or wanting more in their life. There are talkers and doers in life. Be a doer, not a talker. If you have come this far in the book, you are a doer. Don't let anything stop you from continuing on this path to another level of life. One of the simple truths I live by today is "Watch what people do, not what they say." We live in a world of great starters and few finishers. If you're one of those rare people who commit to do something, then also commit to finish and follow through. When you do, you'll stand head and shoulders above the rest—and in the top 10% of society.

Seeds of Greatness

"You can't have the fruits without the roots.
It's the principle of sequencing:
Private Victories precede Public Victories.
Self mastery and self-discipline are
the foundation of good relationships with others."
—Stephen Covey

The overwhelming majority of the world just talks about making a changes in their lives, but they don't do anything about it. Well, guess what? You did. You took that first step, or you wouldn't be reading this far.

I made up a story one day while I was onstage giving a presentation. A man in the audience was telling me that he had tried a million different things, yet had no success. From what he shared with me, I could tell his lack of success sprang from his lack of follow-through. He was repeating the same steps with everything he tried and getting the same results. Well, the story I told affected him and the rest of attendees so greatly that I now tell it to people whenever I can.

Imagine two neighbors. You give each a pack of the same tomato seeds. You say to them, "Here is your goal. I want you to stay focused and make it happen. I want you to grow big, beautiful tomatoes by the end of the season."

Neighbor 1 grabs the seeds, walks out in his backyard, kicks over some dirt, and finds a little open spot. He rips open the bag of tomato seeds with his teeth, and dumps them in one pile. He kicks some dirt over them and goes back inside the house. He grabs a beer and watches TV.

Neighbor 2 reads the directions. He gets a hoe, finds a spot in the sun that makes sense, and hoes up the ground. He plants the seeds carefully, and puts some fertilizer on them. He waters them and takes care of them. If weeds start to grow, he pulls them. If the vines get long and limber, he stakes them.

...doing what needs to be done for success, not just hoping it will happen.

Neighbor 1 walks outside every once in a while. He scratches his head and looks at the tomatoes coming up and says, "Ah, they're growing," and then he goes back inside. Neighbor 2 is focusing on making it happen. He is doing what needs to be done for success, not just hoping it will happen.

At the end of the season, Neighbor 1 has a couple of scrawny little tomato plants sticking out of the ground with a couple of green little tomatoes on them, while Neighbor 2 has a beautiful garden full of red, beautiful tomatoes. Why? Because he set a goal to make it happen and went for it, while Neighbor 1 did not. Neighbor 1 went through the motions, but wasn't committed to massive success.

Here is the tragedy of the story. Do you know what Neighbor 1 would say if he had peeked his head over the fence and saw the big, beautiful tomatoes that Neighbor 2 had? He would say, "Neighbor 2 got better seeds than I did"; the natural reaction of someone who is not a doer is to blame lack of success on the materials or another person. He did not take action with what he had in front of him, and guess what? He got bad results. And if this is how Neighbor 1 handled the rest of his life, what kind of results do you think he got?

The opportunity to create a Totally Fulfilled life is right in front of you. You have the seeds. It's all about *what you are going to do with them*. I want to help you as much as I can and help you develop a core that is built for success in all areas of your life. Now it's your turn to take action, plant your seeds of greatness, and make sure they grow.

Chapter Check

- ❑ For most people traditional goal setting doesn't work.

- ❑ Jumping in with both feet before doing some planning can work—sometimes.

- ❑ The first step in achieving is knowing the reason why you have that desire.

- ❑ You don't always have to be right; you just have to be right once at the right time and place.

Chapter

22

Discover the Reason Behind Your Goals

"Goals are incredibly important…or impotent.
You decide."
—Doug Firebaugh

One thing we didn't talk about yet that is critical for success is the reason why you want your goal. Show me a man or woman with great accomplishments, and I'll show you someone with a big "Why"—a big reason to achieve his or her goals.

This is something I still work on every day, because in changing times, and with the drive to go to another level, it's easy to lose sight of what's important. Like I said in the introduction to this book, you need to change your core way of handling life in order to accomplish all you want and have it be long-lasting. You also need to know why you want to do it or you will get temporary changes. You want permanent success. The simplest way to do that is to spend a little time finding your true purpose for wanting a better life. To just say "I want more" or "I deserve more" is not good enough.

Without a purpose behind goals, they are nothing more than words.

If we let outside events determine our reason, we might as well be on a roller coaster. Your goals will change with the wind. Reasons are the roots to long-term success. Therefore, you need to reach deep inside and find the real reason behind everything you want to do or have. Without a purpose behind goals, they are nothing more than words.

If you get too wrapped up in any one thing, it will determine your mood, your happiness, and your destiny. I am so attached to my businesses that sometimes when things are not going as planned, I can start to feel sorry for myself, depressed, and overwhelmed. That is when I have to take a time-out and remember why I am doing all this. I'm not talking about the superficial things; I'm talking about what makes Dean Graziosi have a reason for wanting a life Totally Fulfilled. Getting back to basics and thinking this way gets me back on track.

With a strong motivating reason behind your goals, you will be able to handle the ups and downs in the superficial world, because you have purpose for why you are doing what you do. You can set and accomplish all the goals you want. Without a reason or a purpose, you will feel empty even when you achieve a goal.

Let's make it simple to find the reason you want your life to evolve. If something in your life is not working, it can be downright painful. The hurt of a bad situation is obviously the complete opposite of an ideal situation. We all want to be happy and don't want to be sad. Pretty simple, isn't it?

"When Andrew Carnegie died they discovered a sheet of paper upon which he had written one of the major goals of his life; to spend the first half of his life accumulating money and to spend the last half of his life giving it all away. And he did!"
—Jim Rohn

Think of the things you do in life. The main reasons why you do them are to be happy and avoid getting hurt or feeling sad. So those are driving forces of life. You need to harness that as the "reason" for follow-through on goals. You need to find specific things that make you who you are, that truly satisfy the inner you, that make you feel happy, and that give you a feeling of peace.

These are not superficial things that make you happy, but that give you driving, lifelong happiness. Going to a comedy show may make you laugh, but it's not what truly makes you happy or what you really enjoy as a life situation. Think as hard as you can about what makes you who you are.

Think back to a time in your life when you felt at peace, truly happy, and enjoyed what you were doing. When was it? What were you doing? Where were you? Think back to even when you were a kid. What did you fantasize about doing or being?

Think about the things that really hit home and bring you ultimate happiness in your life. What would you enjoy doing if you could do anything in your life? What makes you feel good? Even though you probably have amazing people in your life, at this point let's just focus on *you*. Think of the big things. Dig deep inside. Even if they are buried by today's pressures and stress, they are in there, and we need to dig them out.

Let me give you a list of my personal examples that help drive me through thick and thin. Hopefully these inspire you to create your own list. These examples are in no particular order; they are just what comes to mind when I really think about what makes me *me*.

◆ Giving to others

◆ Stability and a sense of security for me and the people I love

◆ Accomplishment—I complete any task that I set my mind on, even in the eye of adversity

◆ Loving unconditionally

◆ Being loved unconditionally

- ◆ Family

- ◆ Exploring my spirituality and relationship with God.

- ◆ Being around positive people who make me feel good

- ◆ Being honest and a man of my word

- ◆ Living with integrity

- ◆ Finding solutions

- ◆ Attracting good friends

- ◆ Being a doer, not a talker

- ◆ Being grateful

- ◆ Exploring and traveling

- ◆ Coaching and teaching

These examples help me find the strength to get through tough times and stay focused on who I am and why I want to evolve. Find *your* inner reasons that will drive you to make your ambitions and goals become realities. Take a minute and write down your own list of the things that really make you feel good. Find out what really makes you tick!

Use the space below to do a quick list or you can go to page 283 for more space:

_____

_____

_____

_____

_____

_____

_____

From List to Life

Now I'm going to show you how to take your list and convert it into today's world. For example, if you have written down that you are a people person, you love to explore, and you love to learn new things, but you work in an office doing the same thing every day, you have no one to talk to, and you are not making enough money to travel further than your backyard, then you have a problem. Your day-to-day life goes totally against what you're passionate about.

This simple exercise should help remind you of who you really are and what your reason for wanting more out of life is—your purpose and reason for being on this earth. God (or whoever you believe in) put us here for a reason. What is your reason?

What you wrote down previously, if you truly dug deep inside of yourself, are the things that make you happy and hopefully will allow you to see what your true purpose is. It can help you see that your current exterior life may be in total conflict with the person on the inside—the person you were meant to be. In fact let's take it a step further and create a comparison chart between what truly makes you happy and your present reality. You can create your comparison chart on page 284 or print one out at our web site, www.totallyfulfilled.com. It will only take a moment to do but can be a heck of an eye opener on why you are not fulfilled.

Here is an example of one that may spark some thoughts when creating your own. Remember to use the core attributes you listed above that made you feel good inside and what truly makes you feel like the person you are meant to be.

Present Reality	Totally Fulfilled Self
In Debt	Financially independent
Renting	Owning a home
'96 Ford Taurus	BMW 530i
Few friends	More active social life
Stressed	Worry-free
Paralegal	Entrepreneur

Feel free to make your list more detailed. The more you tailor it to your specific current situation and desires the more action it will cause you to want to take.

You already have everything you need to be a success in any area you choose.

Now if your true purpose and current reality are similar, then congratulations—you are among the very few and by taking the time to examine yourself, you will stay on that path of fulfillment throughout your entire life. But if your true purpose and the things that make you feel good are in complete opposition of your present reality, then congratulations for identifying the problem and taking the time to observe, in black and white, why you're not as fulfilled as you should be. Isn't it amazing how some simple things that can seem like a waste of time could possibly help you see the small steps you need to take to start feeling better each day and get you on the path to a passionate life? You already have everything you need to be a success in any area you choose. I hope that I can encourage you to start the transformation today!

Remember, this book is not about overnight changes. It is about creating a core of success that will allow you to find your groove, your purpose, and set goals that will allow you to lead a totally fulfilled life.

If you were on your deathbed and an angel came down from heaven and said: "You've been given another shot at this. You can come back and be anybody you'd want to be, who would you pick? Michael Jordan? Oprah Winfrey? Brad Pitt? Julia Roberts? Robert Redford? Gandhi? Moses? Martin Luther King? Babe Ruth? Who would you pick?

My greatest goal is for you to look in the mirror and say: "I'd pick *me* at my full potential." No one could even come close to being you at your full potential!

The challenge is that we only get one chance at this. We live in a world filled with fear and insecurity. But I'm here to tell you: You're good enough. It's time to live and leave your legacy. Make your life a masterpiece and live at your full potential.

Keep your purpose with you at all times. Use it as a reference to stay on track and guide you to make the right decisions. Remember your purpose, because soon we are going to make a real simple goal list. This, along with everything else in this book, will be your fuel and driving force for making things happen.

...have people in your life who are your driving force...

In addition to your internal motivation, you have people in your life who are your driving force for wanting more. Maybe it's your kids, husband, wife, or that someone special. Maybe your driving force is proving something to your parents, your family, or your friends. When added to your main "reason," this can be the last piece of motivation you need to make things happen.

Realize that none of these things alone will allow you to have complete fulfillment, because you are doing it for someone else. When you have your personal purpose figured out, then bringing about the things you want for everyone around you will become ten times easier. You will have more of you to give, and you'll be able to do so with a smile and confidence that will make everyone around you shine.

Chapter Check

❏ List *your* inner reasons that will drive you to make your ambitions and goals become realities.

❏ Saying "I want more" or "I deserve more" will not get you more—except more disappointment or frustration.

❏ Understand the reasons why you have the goals and desires you have.

❏ List the motivations that drive you to succeed.

❏ Think about the other people who matter in your life and who depend upon your success.

❏ When your personal purpose and your motivations unite, you can accomplish anything.

Chapter 23

Let Go of Your Past

"If you look at what you have in life,
You'll always have more.
If you look at what you don't have in life,
You'll never have enough."
—Oprah Winfrey

A well-known speaker started off his seminar by holding up a $20 bill. In the room of 200, he asked, "Who would like this $20 bill?" Hands started going up.

He said, "I am going to give this $20 to one of you but first, let me do this." He proceeded to crumple the $20 dollar bill up. He then asked, "Who still wants it?" Still the hands were up in the air. "Well", he replied, "What if I do this?" And he dropped it on the ground and started to grind it into the floor with his shoe. He picked it up, now crumpled and dirty. "Now who still wants it?"

Still the hands went into the air. "My friends, we have all learned a very valuable lesson", he said, "No matter what I did to the money, you still wanted it because it did not decrease in value. It was still worth $20.

Many times in our lives, we are dropped, crumpled, and ground into the dirt by the decisions we make and the circumstances that come our way. We feel as though we are worthless. But no matter what has happened or what will happen, you will never lose your value. Dirty or clean, crumpled or finely creased, you are still priceless.... and especially to those who love you.

The worth of our lives comes not in what we do or whom we know, but by WHO WE ARE.

"You are special—Don't EVER forget it."

Set Yourself Free

We had an entire chapter on limited beliefs, but I need to revisit and break down a few pieces of that in this chapter. In order to set goals for your future that will stick, there is a very important piece that is a must. *You have let go of your past.* If your past does not serve a greater purpose for the future, then you have to let it go. Even if you feel you are facing a hopeless situation, or you've had things happen to you that have possibly ruined your life forever, you have to realize it is just what it is: the past. Your past can only hurt or stop future growth if you allow it. The past does not equal the future. You are what you focus on.

The past does not equal the future.

We all have had things in our life that have been devastating. Yet, if we hold on, harbor them, and repeat them, then tragedy will live with us forever, never leaving room for growth and prosperity. Are you in the habit of saying or thinking words like, "Why does this always happen to me?" "If I didn't have bad luck I would have no luck at all!" "I would have made it if_____ didn't happen to me," or do you blame someone like an ex-spouse, ex-business partner, or even a family member for your problems?

If you sit around with people and compete to see who has the worst problems, you will get what you focus on: more problems. Your past could quite possibly be the anchor keeping your ship from sailing. What you focus on comes true, so be careful what you think about on a steady basis. This may seem harsh, but there is no room in a fulfilled life for feeling sorry for yourself.

Imagine how silly you would sound if you were sitting with God after your life was over, and you were explaining why your life was so unfulfilled. When He asked you why, you said, "Because my parents were tough on me." I think God would reply, "You have to be kidding me. You moved out of the house when you were 18. What the heck did they have to do with the next 20, 30, 40 or even 60 years?" It's foolish to hold on to that way of thinking, wouldn't you agree?

If someone did you wrong, and you are still holding the anger, you're only hurting yourself. You need to let go of it. Take a walk, and scream out loud if you have to, and release the past. It's not serving you. **What happened yesterday is done and over. It's time to focus on tomorrow.** Refuse to make excuses about your future based on the past. It's the only way to live a life Totally Fulfilled.

> *If someone did you wrong, and you are still holding the anger, you're only hurting yourself.*

If you continue to allow the past to hurt your future, you are reliving that situation over and over, causing the future to be just like the past. You are reading this book to make a new future, not to keep living a life that is not 100% what you are capable of. I am not trying to make you someone you are not or give you a special widget for happiness. Rather, I am here to help you replenish your juice for life in a way you never thought possible. So stay with me.

Think about it. Why can some people face so much adversity and bounce back with a positive attitude and ten times stronger than before? It's not because their problems were easier than other people's. Rather, they made a decision not to allow the past to determine their future. They took what they had and made the most of it. They made a decision that even though their past was difficult; they were not going to use it as a crutch for the future.

Do you have a crutch? If so, let's get rid of it; let's change it! Don't look back when you are nearing the end of your life and have a mound of regrets. In fact, here is a great example of perspective. Think about how you would feel in the following situations:

- Failed in business at age 31.
- Defeated in a legislative race at age 32.
- Failed again in business at age 34.
- Overcame the death of his sweetheart at age 35.
- Had a nervous breakdown at age 36.
- Lost an election at age 38.
- Lost a congressional race at age 43.
- Lost another congressional race at age 48.
- Lost a senatorial race at age 55.
- Failed to become vice president at age 56.
- Lost another senatorial race at age 58.

By the way, how are we doing so far? Is this person doomed, or what? What's your take? Do you like the underdog? Me, too.

In conclusion…

He was elected president of the United States at age 60. His name was Abraham Lincoln.

Do what other people do and you can achieve what they have.

Can you imagine facing adversity so often? What made the difference? The exact tools you are being provided in this book. Do what other people do and you can achieve what they have. This isn't something I dreamed up to sell books; it's how life works.

You have all the tools to achieve massive success. It's your time to shine.

Appreciate the Lessons

Here is another example that may help you when you are wondering if you should make a move towards a new life. When I was growing up, living with my grandmother, and I was worried, my Gram used to say, "Dean, I was your age yesterday, and now I am an old woman. Don't be my age and regret wasting even a second of your life on negative things. Go for what you want and realize that so many things that people worry about in life end up meaning nothing when you look back. Cherish every day."

My Grandmother has Alzheimer's now, and we can't communicate anymore. I miss her so much. Her simple wisdom and our friendship will last an eternity. I will be forever grateful she was such a special part of my life.

It's all how we choose to "see it." For example, I could take my grandmother's illness two ways. I could be bitter and ask God, "Why would you do this to such an amazing lady who had such a tough time in life, who gave to so many people and asked for nothing back?" I could be bitter, resentful, and spiteful about the situation. But I am not.

As I write this, a feeling of warmth washes over me because I don't ask "Why." I have come to realize her words were so much stronger than I ever imagined, even in illness and someday death. I understand I can't spend even a second on the things I can't change. I can thank God, and I can focus on how fortunate I was to have her in my life. A big reason I am the man I am today is because of her.

I think of the amazing time I got to spend with her, and the lessons that will make tomorrow better than yesterday. I lived with her for much of my childhood. Her house was the safe house for me. When I lived with Gram, she always took the time to encourage me to be better. She told me that I was gorgeous every day, even when I was a buck-toothed kid. If I told her I wanted to build a spaceship and go to Mars she would answer: "What parts do we need to get you started on your ship?" She allowed me to not have limitations. She helped build my confidence when I was a very shy boy. She allowed me to dream. She was my Gram, my friend, my inspiration, and my mentor. How could I view her life for even one second as a negative? It would go against everything I am and everything she helped me to be.

As I write this section, it has only been a few days since I got back from Virginia, where my grandmother now lives. She is not in the best of health and can barely speak. When she does speak, she is confused. But I still see the beautiful woman I once knew. I would gladly give up a few years of my life to have the old Gram back. But I can't. Her words will ring in my ears forever. I hope I am able to share this gift with you that will allow some of her words and some of mine to ring in your ears in times of adversity. It's the greatest gift I could give you.

Free Yourself from Ill Thoughts

We all have different aspects of life that can hold us back. I used to hold ill thoughts about some of the choices my parents made. How could each of my parents get married four times and still be single? Why did my dad have a problem with anger and cause me so much stress when I was young? Why did my grandfather, who was like a second dad to me, die when I was ten? Why did my mom move away when I was twelve and we only got to see each other a few times a year? Like you, I could ask why. I choose not to. Those experiences helped create the person I am today. And I like me!

Use your past experiences as a springboard for greater success, not a reason to fail.

Use your past experiences as a springboard for greater success, not a reason to fail. I'm definitely not perfect and have lots of room to grow, but I am proud of the things I have accomplished.

I'm thankful I have the opportunity to re-invent myself every day if I so choose.

You can choose to allow your past to hold you back, or you can make a decision to appreciate every experience you have had. Today you get to take control and change. If you take things that at one time you had an ill thought towards and spin them to empower you, then you will have sense of inner peace that no money could ever buy.

So let's be thankful for our past, good or bad. And let's take anything you may harbor as a crutch and turn it into a positive thought that can help serve you on your journey. Embrace this incredible gift of being thankful. Here are a few that come to mind for me:

- I am so thankful that I had my grandmother in my life and for the lifelong gifts she gave me.

- I am so grateful that my mother showed me how to be compassionate to others and how to say "I love you" without hesitation.

- Thank you, Dad, for teaching me a strong work ethic and allowing me to learn through trial and error and not just words. You always allowed me to tell the truth, no matter what it was. That is a lesson that will last a lifetime.

- I am thankful to God for the amazing people that have come in and out of my life, and for giving me the skills to overcome obstacles and focus on solutions, and for allowing me to accomplish anything I put my mind to.

- I am thankful for every single person who has come into my life and the unique relationships I have shared with them. Each and every person has in one way or another affected my life, and I am grateful for that.

Try it. It feels good. It can truly give you inspiration towards tomorrow. It's time to move through the limits and reach your full potential. We could all yell out loud the things that we are not grateful for, but how in the world could that serve our future? It can't.

Forgive Yourself

The final thing we must do to create the path for lasting change and set goals that will stick is to forgive ourselves. We all make mistakes. I wish I could go back and change decisions I made in my life that affected other people negatively. But I can't. I can only forgive myself. Sometimes the hardest person to forgive is yourself.

Sometimes the person hardest to forgive is yourself.

We talked a lot about the tools that will help you create a "core" that will allow you to do anything. If there is anything inside of you that haunts you from your past—something you may be ashamed of like ending a relationship, committing a crime, being unfaithful, doing drugs, drinking too much, ignoring someone when they needed you, making a bad business decision, and 100 other things—you may feel some guilt. That guilt could be the very thing that is holding you back from a better tomorrow. Realize that today can be a fresh start. If you are one of the many people who believe in God, and if you repent your sins and are truly sorry for them, then God will forgive you and fill you with love. If God can forgive you, follow that example and forgive yourself. While you are at it, forgive anyone who may have wronged you.

You are judged more on what you do after you make a mistake than on the mistake itself. So you can dwell on the mistake, allowing it to paralyze your future, or you can use it as motivation to fuel your future.

For example, if you messed up on a relationship and it pains you to think about it, dig deep inside and think about what went wrong. It may hurt because it was 75% your fault. But learn from it and make sure you don't do it again. Don't focus on things you can't change. Rather, set a goal for a fresh start because you deserve it. Give yourself permission to let go of past mistakes. Look towards the future, knowing you are one step closer to a life Totally Fulfilled, focused on growing, learning, and living a better life.

You have the power inside of you to live the life you were meant to live. Isn't it time to give yourself that gift?

Chapter Check

❑ No matter what you've experienced in the past, you still have value.

❑ No matter what people have told you about yourself in the past, you still have value.

❑ No matter what mistakes you've made in the past, you still have value.

❑ You are a valuable opportunity waiting to take a chance on.

❑ What you did in the past, felt about yourself in the past, and feared in the past, is exactly that—in the past.

❑ Forgive Yourself.

Chapter 24

Reason + Goals - Obstacles = Results

"My own experience has taught me this:
if you wait for the perfect moment when all is safe
and assured, it may never arrive. Mountains will not
be climbed, races won, or lasting happiness achieved."
—Maurice Chevalier

By now, you realize I was serious about not writing down some goals on a piece of paper and hoping they might come true. The goals would be empty and a waste of time. The evolution of this entire book is about building the blocks to set goals that will happen. This is serious. This is real. This is your life we are talking about, and it's time to make a change.

Finding your reason *why* and using the principles in this book make the goal itself really insignificant. Once you have the reason why you want it, you can build a core with all the tools I have given you. Any goal you plug into your core formula is possible.

Here's a secret: Find the reason. Find the goal.

It's time to lay out the road map for your future. Most people spend more time planning grocery and holiday gift shopping lists than designing a life. This is going to be fun, light, and focused at the same time. If you follow my steps, achieving goals will be easy for you.

Think about all you've learned up to this point. Reflect on what you have read on turning limited beliefs into empowering, limitless thinking, how to turn obstacles into welcomed challenges, and how to embrace change as a positive force in your life. We have broken down the core aspects of taking all your relationships to a new level to create a supporting cast. You possess the qualities of a champion and can now pull them out for the world to see. You have a Higher Power standing beside you every step of the way. You are not in this alone. If anything in your past does not serve your future, you have complete control to throw it away. The past, negativity, and the "poor me" syndrome must go down the toilet. You can now move beyond a limited life to accomplish anything you set your mind to. The bigger the "reason," the greater the chance you'll accomplish your goal. It's time to set some goals and live a life Totally Fulfilled.

> *"He who cherishes a beautiful vision, a lofty ideal in his heart, will one day realize it. Dream lofty dreams, and as you dream, so shall you become."*
> —James Allen

The things I have asked you to imagine up to this point may have been a bit limited, because we have only discussed main topics: money, health, relationships, etc. As we approach the end of this journey we now need to get your personal goals down on paper. So you can go to the web site and print out a goal sheet, or go to page 285. I really don't care what you use, but we need to take the time to do this; I promise this is going to get fun. Once you're ready, write down everything you would love to happen in your life. It could be goals for today, tomorrow, next year, or even twenty years from now. Set no limits on your goals. Don't think about how you are going to obtain them. Think only of what you want.

Write down everything that comes to mind—without limits. Reach deep inside of you and dream like you're a kid again. Think how

Reach deep inside of you and dream like you're a kid again.

these goals would make you feel and find the reason why you want them. Don't hold back. There are no boundaries. Just write.

You may have lots of goals, and that's perfect. This is just the practice of writing them all down. Remember the different areas of your life and how you see yourself in the future.

Maybe I can help spark some goals you may not be thinking of.

◆ Do you have any spiritual goals? Do you want to find the right church for you and your family? Do you want to get closer to God? Do you want to read the Bible?

◆ What are your self-improvement goals? Do you want to spend more time with family? Stop smoking? Learn a new trade? Be more confident? Stop procrastinating? Become an action-oriented person? Become a problem solver rather than a problem talker? Be more grateful?

◆ What about your body and health? Do you want to get through an illness? Do you want to lose weight? Eat healthier? Exercise? Be physically fit?

◆ How do you want to feel on a daily basis? Grateful? Happy? Confident? Accomplished? Powerful? Relaxed? In control? Secure? At ease? What would your mental health be like?

◆ How would you like your current relationships to evolve? What new relationships would you like to come into your life? Who would you hang around? Which family members would you spend more time with? What people would you spend less time with? Would you like to get married? Have children?

◆ Would you like to live in another state or even another country?

◆ What kind of career goals do you have? Do you want a new job? A raise? Do you want to retire? Change careers? How would your finances be? Would you be earning ten times as much as you do now? Would you work fewer hours for more money? Would you own your own business and have the freedom to make your own decisions? What would you buy? Who would you help with the money? What charity would you contribute to? Maybe you want enough money for a dream home or money for retirement or a college fund for your children?

◆ What fun things would you like to have? Do you want to skydive? Take more vacations? Buy a snowmobile, jet ski, or boat? Would you take up golf and join a country club? Would you drive a racecar? Go on a safari?

You should have a variety of goals. Some may be life-saving, some life-changing, some very serious, and others could be simply fun. Did it feel good to think of the ideal life with your personal goals coming true? If you can only think of a few goals, dig deeper.

Now that you have this great list of things that would be amazing for you, I want you to know that everything on your list is possible. Be realistic about the starting point. I want to steer you away from feeling overwhelmed and put you on a path of fun and easy enjoyment. Now that you have all these goals written down, I have another exercise I want you to do for me now.

Imagine you found a magic lamp. When you rubbed the lamp, a genie appeared. The genie said, "Thank you for releasing me from this lamp. For that I am going to grant you ten wishes. The first three wishes will happen over the next six months." Right now, go through your goal list and find the three most important goals that will improve your life within the next six months and put a number one next to them. Really think about it because you only have three to choose from, and you may have twenty, fifty, or more goals on your list. So choose wisely. Remember, this is not an exercise to figure out how you are going to reach these goals right now; rather, it's just about setting them.

Next, the genie says, "Your next three wishes are things that will happen over the next 18 months." So look hard at your list and pick three more and put a number 2 next to them. Finally, the Genie says, "Your last three wishes are things that will happen over the next five to ten years." So choose wisely. Go to your list and put a number 3 next to these goals.

Now you have nine wishes marked accordingly from your master sheet. Stay with me on my silly genie analogy; it's going to come to life soon. It's the road map for the new direction your life is going to take, and right now you have the power to set a new course.

Then the Genie says: "Now the nine wishes you've chosen must be very important to your life and your fulfillment. They are probably wishes for you and the people you love, and may even involve some serious changes that need to happen in your life. For your tenth and final wish I need you to go to your goal list and pick ten other goals: fun goals. These may be wishes you had as a child—things that you want to happen over the next couple of years. These are important to you, but they are more fun than serious." Put a bullet point or check mark next to these goals.

Finally, Genie looks at you and says, "There is only one stipulation. Using everything you have learned by reading *Totally Fulfilled*, I want you to write one to two sentences under each wish (goal) with the reason behind the wish (goal) along with the feelings it will give you once you achieve it. If you do not dig deep enough to find the true meaning and feelings of your wish (goal), it will not be granted to you. So please find the reason behind it. Write wisely."

As you go through each of the goals in the exercise, you will likely find similar reasons and feelings associated with several of them. That's okay. Just keep writing the reason and the feelings you will get as each one becomes a reality. So go to page 289 or use another piece of paper or print it out at the web site and write down your goals in priority with the reason you want it and the feelings it will give you once it is accomplished.

For example if your wish is:

◆ I want to find my soul mate and get married.

Your reasons may be:

◆ I am a loving, caring person and I want to share my life with another. I enjoy companionship and love and I am not meant to be alone. I also love children and that is something I want to fulfill.

Feelings I will get once my goal is achieved:

◆ Love, security, a sense of peace, strength, respect, stability, joy and happiness.

Now, as silly as the genie analogy may have been, if you did it, it has led you to truly figure out what you want and why you want it. It's your time to live a life on FIRE! As you evolve, grow, and develop, so will your goals. Goals you set today may seem funny compared to the goals you set a year from now. Once you have this list ironed out, write them on a clean piece of paper and carry them with you wherever you go. Maybe you put it in your notebook, day-planner, or on your desktop. Put them someplace you can access often. When you need a reminder, simply go back to the basics to get on track. Remember to actually visualize your goals being accomplished even before they are and allow yourself to *feel* the emotions in anticipation of what you will feel once your goals are accomplished. Let those emotions always serve as your fuel towards the life you are supposed to be living.

It's your time to live a life on FIRE!

Every six months revisit these goals and let them evolve with you. If you want to use my silly analogy, then get the genie to come and see you every six months to grant you a new list of wishes. If you truly follow everything we discussed, you'll realize that these are not just wishes. You will unlock the door to prosperity, wealth, and abundance. You will learn how to create your future.

> *"Nothing is as real as a dream.*
> *The world can change around you,*
> *but your dream will not.*
> *Responsibilities need not erase it.*
> *Duties need not obscure it.*
> *Because the dream is within you; no one can take it away."*
> —Tom Clancy

By now you likely feel excited about your future possibilities. You feel unstoppable. That's great! As you let these feelings take over, remember the process we just outlined.

Chapter Check

1. Develop goals with reason.

2. Let go of your past if it does not serve you.

3. Become a doer.

4. Be grateful.

5. Forgive yourself and others.

6. Write a list of the things you love to do and the person you love to be.

7. Write a list of ALL the goals you want to achieve.

8. Rub the Genie's lamp and pick your top nine goals and write the reasons why you must achieve them.

9. To assist you in the process, I invite you to go www.totallyfulfilled.com to get your FREE tools to help guide you and keep you on track.

By following this process, your goals now have life. Congratulations! It's time to celebrate the brand new YOU!

Section Summary:

- ❑ For most people traditional goal setting doesn't work.

- ❑ Jumping in with both feet before doing some planning can work—sometimes.

- ❑ The first step in achieving is knowing the reason why you have that desire.

- ❑ You don't always have to be right; you just have to be right once at the right time and place.

- ❑ Saying "I want more" or "I deserve more" will not get you more—except more disappointment or frustration.

- ❑ Understand the reasons why you have the goals and desires you have.

- ❑ List the motivations that drive you to succeed.

- ❑ Think about the other people who matter in your life and who depend upon your success.

- ❑ When your personal purpose and your motivations unite, you can accomplish anything.

- ❑ No matter what you've experienced in the past, you still have value.

- ❑ No matter what people have told you about yourself in the past, you still have value.

- ❑ No matter what mistakes you've made in the past, you still have value.

❑ You are a valuable opportunity waiting to take a chance on.

❑ What you did in the past, felt about yourself in the past, and feared in the past, is exactly that—in the past.

❑ Forgive Yourself.

Part 6

Chapter 25

A Life Totally Fulfilled

> *"We never know how high we are*
> *Till we are called to rise;*
> *And then, if we are true to plan,*
> *Our statures touch the skies."*
> —Emily Dickinson

Congratulations for coming this far. You are among the minority. Statistically, more people will quit reading any book halfway through than complete the book. In most cases, it has nothing to do with the book's content; rather, it boils down to the person's commitment to finish.

At this point, you probably feel one of two ways. Maybe you see the potential of your life, and you are experiencing a rush of confidence, happiness, joy, enthusiasm, love, freedom, and fun using the proven principles I've shared with you. We all love to

> *People will always be more impressed with the height of your passion and enthusiasm than the depth of your knowledge.*

hang around people who have those traits, and you are becoming the person that people will be attracted to because of your passion for life, your ability to overcome obstacles, and your confidence about focusing on solutions. People will always be **more impressed** with the height of your passion and enthusiasm than the depth of your knowledge.

Expanding Your Comfort Zone

But you could also be feeling a bit uncomfortable with the changes you feel you need to make. Well, that feeling is just as good as the first one. Why? Because it means that what I am sharing with you is working; it's sinking in and taking effect. It is evoking feelings and making you analyze your life. You're realizing that it's time to make a change and live the best life you can right now.

Look at it this way. You have been living the same life for twenty, thirty, forty, sixty, or even eighty years. Introducing a new way of thinking may stretch you and your comfort zone. This is the time to confirm that something in your life to this point has been missing. So if you are unsure, uneasy, or uncomfortable, it's okay. That means positive change is on the way. You have all the tools. Now it's time to start, even if it's with baby steps.

Let's compare this situation to a golfer who was self-taught and using the same swing for twenty years. His game may be good. He can play without being embarrassed, but he wants to improve and play golf on another level. However, he feels it may be impossible since he has played for twenty years and not improved. The reason he can't get better is not because he doesn't practice. It's because he is practicing the wrong way. So the golfer decides to take lessons from a golf pro.

When he goes for the lesson, the pro changes the way the golfer stands, holds the club, and swings. This golfer of twenty years feels totally uncomfortable, like he's starting all over again. And the first day he can barely hit the ball. He is in an all-time level of discomfort when it comes to his golf swing. But guess what? The golf pro is giving him the proper way to practice—*like this book is doing for your life.*

The golfer can make one of two decisions: 1) He can work through the uncomfortable feelings, learn from someone who plays the way he wishes he could play, and inevitably get better than he ever has been in his life. Or, 2) he can retreat back to what he knew—his old stance and old swing—and inevitably play a mediocre game of golf for the rest of his life.

Isn't this exactly how life is? At this point, you can either put the book down and go back to the life you had, or you can work through any discomfort and make a lasting change. If you bought this book and have come this far, chances are your "Life" game is not where you want it to be. Most likely, no one ever showed you a better way… until now. So you can decide to retreat to the life you had which may not have been great but was comfortable, or *right now*, at this very second, you can decide that even though it may be a little uncomfortable at first, you are going to take the lessons you have learned, apply them, and win at the game of life. Play at a level you deserve, a level other people achieve every day, by practicing and improving upon the right techniques, not the wrong ones.

I hope this book made you uncomfortable about areas of your life that are not fulfilled, and that it excited you on a new level because of the endless possibilities available to you. If you learn how to play the game of life by modeling those who are winning at it, then it is just a matter of time before you are victorious.

Chapter Check

❑ People will always be more impressed with the height of your enthusiasm than the depth of your knowledge.

❑ Being stretched outside your comfort zone can be uncomfortable.

❑ You have a choice to make between striving for lasting change or staying the same.

❑ Now that you've been shown a better way, you can model your life after those who are Totally Fulfilled.

Chapter 26

Putting It All Together

"You may be disappointed if you fail,
but you are doomed if you don't try!"
—Beverly Sills

In today's world, there is either a pill for everything that ails you or a guru for that specific category you feel less than fulfilled in. No wonder most people feel overwhelmed. And people are making a fortune from this because most consumers don't have the core it takes to get things accomplished.

Because people don't have the proper skills to be successful, companies will continue to sell everything under the sun for self improvement that will never work. It's not necessarily that the product does not work, but that people don't have follow through. They want the quick fix. In fact, companies count on you not succeeding. It's called "breakage."

If everyone had follow-through, then a lot of these companies would go out of business. So what does that tell you? That there really is no magic pill, no get rich quick opportunities, no magical relationship seminar to save a marriage, no patch to make you quit smoking, no special workout that will make you thin in just weeks. If you don't have the core success principles that I have shared with you in this book, nothing will ever work, long term.

Once you take the time to build the right core, then anything you want to achieve is possible. You create the core by adopting new limitless beliefs, overcoming obstacles, and embracing change. You have sound relationship skills for success, and you have a proven system for setting goals and making them happen.

Really think about how you have evolved throughout this book. Think about all the things you want to accomplish, and then think of plugging them into this core I have talked so much about.

Would approaching anything in your life be doable if you addressed each thing with the same success principles that so many people have used for thousands of years? Could your business grow and expand from it? Could your relationships become stronger? Could you be more confident? Could you get a new job or a raise? Could you get healthier? Quit smoking? Start exercising? Start eating healthier? Be the best person you can be on all levels? ABSOLUTELY!

Once you form a solid "core," then success in anything you plug into it is inevitable.

Do you see now why I said right in the beginning that, if approached correctly, all the things you want to accomplish, overcome, or fix are not separate? Once you form a solid "core," then success in anything you plug into it is inevitable.

If you take the time to let these secrets sink in, and you practice them, you will have the ability and the confidence to know that you can truly do anything you want, that you can have anything anyone else has, and that you have the ingredients for a Totally Fulfilled life.

I know many traditionalists in the success field cringe at what I have shared with you. The bottom line is that I have shared *real world information* with you, not some regurgitated psycho-babble. My goal is to take the gift I was blessed with—to go for anything I desire full speed ahead, find what works and does not work along the way—and convert that knowledge into a simple way for you to understand it, digest it, and apply it.

As I have mentioned I have only read a handful of books in my life. I have only attended a handful of seminars in my life, and that was because I spoke at them. But with my very fortunate success, I have had the chance to meet many of the so-called experts ranting and raving about success and their "black and white" approach to it. Quite frankly, many of their opinions drive me nuts. Many seem to be based on a great theory, but not on real life. And many did not seem to be living the successful life they were selling to others. I've found, in the real world of success, happiness, and fulfillment, there is no black or white; rather, it's gray. There are many different paths to success. But having the right "core" is like having a set of maps, all with the correct destination, yet possibly different routes that you can choose to fit you and your life.

And that is my goal: To give you a road map to success. But you have to use it. Once you apply these lessons and see how they work, you will likely refer to this book as your handbook for success. These principles have stood the test of time. I feel confident that I have cut through the fat and gristle to give you the meat of what you need faster and easier.

If you need help staying on course and setting that "core" of success inside of you, then find a mentor who can help you. Find someone who inspires you and keeps you accountable for the evolution of your life. If you don't have a person who can be your mentor to help you stay on track, then go to *www.totallyfulfilled.com* and learn how you can talk to an advisor—at no cost—about your future and possibly get help from one of our mentors, or you could attend one of my FREE Tele-Seminars that could inspire you to stay on track.

This book is everything you need to change your life, but if you want a little help or a jump start, then don't hesitate to let us help. Remember, Knowledge + Action = Results. Knowledge without action is just good reading. Don't let this book be just a good read. Without the core success principles in this book, no change you make will last.

Knowledge + Action = Results

Chapter Check

❑ Once you have the right core, everything else you want to do becomes possible.

❑ You can't be taught to be successful through theory; you have to have real world / practical experiences of doing and trying.

❑ Knowledge + Action = Results

Chapter 27

Making It All Happen

"Your task...to build a better world," God said.
I answered, "How?...this world is such a large, vast place,
and there's nothing I can do."
But God in all His wisdom said, "Just build a better you."
—Author Unknown

I know I mention the word "core" over and over. Why? I can't say it enough: with the right core, you can truly be fulfilled in every area of your life. This is not a new concept. It is the key element that successful, fulfilled people have used for centuries.

I have been fortunate enough to live this way by accident. And through my experiences and trial and error, I hope I have sparked something in you that says, "If he can do it, so can I." You truly have no limits in your life. You are what you focus on, and nothing anyone else in life can accomplish is beyond your capabilities. I hope that my simple twist on it all allows you to digest it and put these proven techniques into effect and start altering your life immediately.

A fulfilled life is not for other people anymore; it's for you, and you deserve it.

You now have built a foundation under your goals. Put another way, you've planted the seeds, pulled the weeds, and developed roots under your tree to grow strong. There is absolutely no reason or excuse from this point on that you can't start making a positive change in all areas of your life. We took a journey to create a "core" that can accomplish anything. A fulfilled life is not for other people anymore; it's for you, and you deserve it. Don't let life pass you by when now you know there is more for you.

Let's do a quick recap:

◆ We acknowledged limiting beliefs and the paralyzing effect they can have on us. You had time to find and identify the limiting beliefs inside you and convert them to empowering "limitless" beliefs. Remember, this is something you will have to stay on top of. Your limiting beliefs will pop back up in your life often. They have been there for a while, so it may take a long time to get rid of them. You have everything you need to overcome them and stay empowered by using your thoughts. Also remember that practicing "the right thing" makes perfect. If you wanted to be a professional cyclist like Lance Armstrong, you wouldn't practice once and expect to be a super star. You would commit to the belief that you will get out there and practice on a regular basis. Living a life Totally Fulfilled can be much easier than winning the Tour De France if you just adapt a few key changes into your life. It starts with the belief that you can do anything you want with no restrictions. You can do it!

◆ We discussed obstacles that most of us face, especially if we want something better for ourselves. These obstacles can make you turn around and retreat to the life you obviously want to change, or they can be nothing more than a challenge or excuse you will overcome. We know now that all of us will have challenges and problems and make mistakes. They won't ever go away, and the more success you have in all areas of your life, the more challenges you will have, too. So we know it's not about stopping challenges; it's about how we handle and overcome them. We know that when a challenge, obstacle, or a problem arises, we should immediately take action to find the solution. Wasting energy on the "Why me?" and "How could this happen?" questions only delays the resolution. When handled correctly, challenges will always result in a building block towards your fulfilled life and success. Don't aim for a mistake, but if you do make one, learn from it, cherish it, and figure out how to keep it from happening again. Now you know there truly are no obstacles in life, just excuses and challenges. And you are strong enough to overcome them both.

◆ We faced change head on—whether it's change you know you need to make or unexpected change. Once you alter your perception of change, you will embrace it, and actually look forward to it because something better is just around the corner. Remember, the definition of insanity is "doing the same thing over and over again expecting a different result." To me, that is also the definition of an unfulfilled life. If your life is not where you would like it to be, if you are unfulfilled in one or more areas of your life, or if you are downright unhappy, then the only way to make something better is to make a **change!**

"The longest journey begins with the first step!"
—Confucius

◆ We talked in depth about the power of communication and relationships as a keystone in the foundation of a fulfilled life. Relationships on all levels can be the wind beneath your wings so you can soar to new heights, or they can be the anchor that weighs you down and keeps you moored in stagnant water. If we take the time to listen to what people say and truly hear them, the magic of a relationship—personal or business—can only grow to new heights. We discussed that one of the most important relationships is the one you have with yourself, and to be true to who you are. Be a person of your word even when it is not convenient. Even though you may have been taken advantage of in the past, giving to others what you would hope to receive is a key factor to total fulfillment. Give and you shall receive—maybe not at that exact moment—but life is not a five-minute game. The rewards can be limitless. We also learned not to let other people's thoughts and words dictate our future or goals. Don't let anyone steal your dreams. *You* are the captain of your ship.

◆ You now have one of the most powerful secrets to success and fulfillment. Setting realistic goals that have meaning behind them, you have found your reason and purpose based on what truly makes you happy inside. You have taken the time to describe the feeling each goal will give you. And those feelings are the pieces that allow dreams to become reality, not a piece of paper hoping to come to life. You can now make a decision on a goal and know that it is not a question of *if* it will come true, but rather *when*. You know now that in order to accomplish your goals, the final piece is not to use your past as an excuse. Forgive yourself and release any guilt you may have, because it does not serve anyone, especially you.

◆ Most important, a key factor to your success is actually putting this information to work. Take action and be a doer. Be the kind of person people look at and wonder where you got the courage, the strength, and the ability to stand out and make things happen. You *are* that type of person. Everyone has it inside. But if you are still here, still reading, then you are in that percentage of doers. You have a road map of your future—a future of passion, prosperity, and purpose, and a life totally fulfilled. So get out there and make it happen!

By going through this process, you have stumbled across the "genie in the bottle" to create the life you desire. The world is waiting for you. It's time to leave your legacy. You may have dreamed of a different destination in the past, but have not been able to get there because you didn't have the right vehicle or directions. Well, my friend, you now have the car, the directions, the gas, two spare tires, and an alternate route if something happens to the first one. The only thing left is to get in the car and start it, put it in drive, and move forward. It's time to put your body, mind, and soul in action and start moving forward towards the life you deserve. It's your life. Seize the day!

Core Attributes of Totally Fulfilled people:

◆ Positive / Optimist

◆ Open Minded

◆ Passionate

◆ Grateful

◆ Imaginative

◆ Responsible

◆ Productive

◆ Money-Wise

◆ Flexible

◆ Active Responders

◆ Forward thinking

Part 7

Chapter 28

Inspiration is Timeless

The day before the final edition of the book went to the press I decided to create this additional section. Why? I was online and saw a quote from Dale Carnegie that was so inspiring and so confirming to the way I think that I had to investigate. I did some research on him that led me down an inspirational path. I already shared this with you so I am not ashamed to say; I have only read a handful of books in my life and I was not the best student in high school. I was fortunate enough to learn techniques for optimal success through trial and error as well as modeling myself after a mentor, when one was available. So up until then I didn't know what Dale Carnegie was all about. I knew about Carnegie Hall, but truthfully that was the extent of my knowledge of the man.

Well, you probably know better than I that Dale Carnegie not only achieved success and fulfillment at amazing levels but also touched the lives of millions of people while doing it. Instead of giving you a biography on Dale Carnegie, I gathered as many quotes as I could find from him that sum up what he was all about. While searching, I also ran across quotes from Benjamin Franklin that I wanted to share with you. The more I searched, the more I was touched by the empowering quotes, short stories and poems that I found. They touched me for one simple reason. You can see that no matter what era they come from, successful people have similar core attributes and beliefs that allow them to excel at higher levels than nearly everyone else.

These messages confirm what I know to be true. That is if you create and adopt these core attributes, any level of success that you want to achieve is possible. Do as they do, say what they say, act as they act and achieve what they have achieved. Folks, I didn't create success or fulfillment, what I have done is create a simple, adaptable model so that anyone can achieve it.

So I took what I found, compiled them in no particular order and got them to the printer at the last minute so I could share them with you.

If I found a story or poem without an author, we searched the internet to find the author so we could give credit where credit was due and thank them. But with some of the stories there was simply no way to find the writer. I chose to print these great messages anyway because I know the authors' intent was to inspire and help others see a path to greatness. So, I say to the creators of any of the following inspirational stories or poems, thank you from all of us.

Remember that technology may change and the world may change, but people don't change. The ones that soar at different levels, the ones we admire in the end, and the ones who make a difference and leave a legacy of greatness took action. They modeled what was already working and went for it. I urge you to do the same. Go for it!

Dale Carnegie Quotes

"The successful man will profit from his mistakes and try again in a different way."

"Don't be afraid to give your best to what seemingly are small jobs. Every time you conquer one it makes you that much stronger. If you do the little jobs well, the big ones will tend to take care of themselves."

"When fate hands us a lemon, let's try to make lemonade."

"You can make more friends in two months by becoming interested in other people than you can in two years by trying to get other people interested in you."

"If you can't sleep, then get up and do something instead of lying there worrying. It's the worry that gets you, not the lack of sleep."

"First ask yourself:
What is the worst that can happen?
Then prepare to accept it.
Then proceed to improve on the worst."

"Be more concerned with your character than with your reputation. Your character is what you really are while your reputation is merely what others think you are."

"Would you sell both your eyes for a million dollars…or your two legs…or your hands…or your hearing? Add up what you do have, and you'll find you won't sell them for all the gold in the world. The best things in life are yours, if you can appreciate them."

"Inaction breeds doubt and fear. Action breeds confidence and courage. If you want to conquer fear, do not sit home and think about it. Go out and get busy."

"Most of the important things in the world have been accomplished by people who have kept on trying when there seemed to be no help at all."

"Do the thing you fear to do and keep on doing it... that is the quickest and surest way ever yet discovered to conquer fear."

"If you want to win friends, make it a point to remember them. If you remember my name, you pay me a subtle compliment; you indicate that I have made an impression on you. Remember my name and you add to my feeling of importance."

"All the king's horses and all the king's men can't put the past together again. So let's remember: Don't try to saw sawdust."

"Are you bored with life? Then throw yourself into some work you believe in with all your heart, live for it, die for it, and you will find happiness that you had thought could never be yours."

"Pay less attention to what men say. Just watch what they do."

"If we think happy thoughts, we will be happy. If we think miserable thoughts, we will be miserable."

"Any fool can criticize, condemn, and complain but it takes character and self-control to be understanding and forgiving."

"Remember happiness doesn't depend upon who you are or what you have; it depends solely on what you think."

"One of the most tragic things I know about human nature is that all of us tend to put off living. We are all dreaming of some magical rose garden over the horizon-instead of enjoying the roses blooming outside our windows today."

Benjamin Franklin Quotes

"Some people die at twenty-five and aren't buried until they are seventy-five."

"Well done, is better than well said."

"We must all hang together, or assuredly, we shall all hang separately."

"He that lives upon hope will die fasting."

"You may delay, but time will not."

"Never leave that till tomorrow which you can do today."

"Be civil to all; sociable to many; familiar with few; friend to one; enemy to none."

"Whatever is begun in anger ends in shame."

"Diligence is the mother of good luck."

"Drive thy business or it will drive thee."

"Write your injuries in dust, your benefits in marble."

"Remember not only to say the right thing in the right place, but far more difficult still, to leave unsaid the wrong thing at the tempting moment."

"Glass, china, and reputation are easily cracked, and never mended well."

"There are two ways of being happy:
We must either diminish our wants or augment our means—either may do—the result is the same and it is for each man to decide for himself and to do that which happens to be easier."

"He that is good for making excuses is seldom good for anything else."

"Do not anticipate trouble, or worry about what may never happen. Keep in the sunlight."

"When you're finished changing, you're finished."

"A spoonful of honey will catch more flies than a gallon of vinegar."

"There never was a good war or a bad peace."

"By failing to prepare you are preparing to fail."

"Being ignorant is not so much a shame as being unwilling to learn."

"Hide not your talents. They for use were made. What's a sundial in the shade."

The World Is Against Me

By Edgar A. Guest

"The world is against me," he said with a sigh.
"Somebody stops every scheme that I try.
The world has me down and it's keeping me there;
I don't get a chance. Oh, the world is unfair!
When a fellow is poor then he can't get a show;
The world is determined to keep him down low."

"What of Abe Lincoln?" I asked. "Would you say
That he was much richer than you are to-day?
He hadn't your chance of making his mark,
And his outlook was often exceedingly dark;
Yet he clung to his purpose with courage most grim
And he got to the top. Was the world against him?"

"What of Ben Franklin? I've oft heard it said
That many a time he went hungry to bed.
He started with nothing but courage to climb,
But patiently struggled and waited his time.
He dangled awhile from real poverty's limb,
Yet he got to the top. Was the world against him?

"I could name you a dozen, yes, hundreds, I guess,
Of poor boys who've patiently climbed to success;
All boys who were down and who struggled alone,
Who'd have thought themselves rich if your fortune they'd known;
Yet they rose in the world you're so quick to condemn,
And I'm asking you now, was the world against them?"

Anything Is Possible

Author Unknown

If there was ever a time to dare,
to make a difference,
to embark on something worth doing,
IT IS NOW.
Not for any grand cause, necessarily...
but for something that tugs at your heart,
something that's your inspiration,
something that's your dream.

You owe it to yourself
to make your days here count.
HAVE FUN.
DIG DEEP.
STRETCH.
DREAM BIG.

Know, though, that things worth doing
seldom come easy.
There will be good days.
And there will be bad days.
There will be times when you want to turn around,
pack it up, and call it quits.
Those times tell you
that you are pushing yourself,
that you are not afraid to learn by trying.

PERSIST.
Because with an idea,
determination, and the right tools,
you can do great things.
Let your instincts, your intellect,
and your heart, guide you.

TRUST.
Believe in the incredible power of the human mind.
Of doing something that makes a difference.
Of working hard.
Of laughing and hoping.
Of lazy afternoons.
Of lasting friends.
Of all the things that will cross your path this year.

The start of something new
brings the hope of something great,
ANYTHING IS POSSIBLE.

The Brick

Author Unknown

A young and successful executive was traveling down a neighborhood street, going a bit too fast in his new Jaguar. He was watching for kids darting out from between parked cars and slowed down when he thought he saw something. As his car passed, no children appeared. Instead, a brick smashed into the Jag's side door! He slammed on the brakes and backed the Jag back to the spot where the brick had been thrown. The angry driver then jumped out of the car, grabbed the nearest kid and pushed him up against a parked car shouting, "What was that all about and who are you? Just what the heck are you doing? That's a new car and that brick you threw is going to cost a lot of money. Why did you do it?"

The young boy was apologetic. "Please, mister...please, I'm sorry but I didn't know what else to do," He pleaded. "I threw the brick because no one else would stop..." With tears dripping down his face and off his chin, the youth pointed to a spot just around a parked car. "It's my brother," he said. "He rolled off the curb and fell out of his wheelchair and I can't lift him up."

Now sobbing, the boy asked the stunned executive, "Would you please help me get him back into his wheelchair? He's hurt and he's too heavy for me."

Moved beyond words, the driver tried to swallow the rapidly swelling lump in his throat. He hurriedly lifted the handicapped boy back into the wheelchair, then took out a linen handkerchief and dabbed at the fresh scrapes and cuts. A quick look told him everything was going to be okay. "Thank you and may God bless you," the grateful child told the stranger. Too shook up for words, the man simply watched the boy push his wheelchair-bound brother down the sidewalk toward their home.

It was a long, slow walk back to the Jaguar. The damage was very noticeable, but the driver never bothered to repair the dented side door. He kept the dent there to remind him of this message: "Don't go through life so fast that someone has to throw a brick at you to get your attention!" God whispers in our souls and speaks to our hearts. Sometimes when we don't have time to listen, He has to throw a brick at us. It's our choice to listen or not.

The Difference Between Winning and Losing

by Catherine Pulsifer

Some of the significant differences between winning and losing are:
Hanging on, persevering,
WINNING
Letting go, giving up easily,
LOSING

Accepting responsibility for your actions,
WINNING
Always having an excuse for your actions,
LOSING

Taking the initiative,
WINNING
Waiting to be told what to do,
LOSING

Knowing what you want and setting goals to achieve it,
WINNING
Wishing for things, but taking no action,
LOSING

Seeing the big picture, and setting your goals accordingly,
WINNING
Seeing only where you are today,
LOSING

Adopt a WINNING attitude!

Don't Quit

Author Unknown

When things go wrong, as they sometimes will,
when the road you're trudging seems all uphill,
when the funds are low and the debts are high,
and you want to smile but you have to sigh,
when care is pressing you down a bit—rest if you must,
but don't you quit.

Life is queer with its twists and turns.
As every one of us sometimes learns.
And many a fellow turns about
when he might have won had he stuck it out.
Don't give up though the pace seems slow—
you may succeed with another blow.

Often the goal is nearer than it seems to a faint and faltering man;
often the struggler has given up
when he might have captured the victor's cup;
and he learned too late when the night came down,
how close he was to the golden crown.

Success is failure turned inside out—
the silver tint of the clouds of doubt,
and when you never can tell how close you are,
it may be near when it seems afar;
so stick to the fight when you're hardest hit—
it's when things seem worst,
you must not quit.

Dare To Be

By Steve Maraboli

When a new day begins,
dare to smile gratefully.

When there is darkness,
dare to be the first to shine a light.

When there is injustice,
dare to be the first to condemn it.

When something seems difficult,
dare to do it anyway.

When life seems to beat you down,
dare to fight back.

When there seems to be no hope,
dare to find some.

When you're feeling tired,
dare to keep going.

When times are tough,
dare to be tougher.

When love hurts you,
dare to love again.

When someone is hurting,
dare to help them heal.

When another is lost,
dare to help them find the way.

When a friend falls,
dare to be the first to extend a hand.

When you cross paths with another,
dare to make them smile.

When you feel great,
dare to help someone else feel great too.

When the day has ended,
dare to feel as you've done your best.

Dare to be the best you can—
At all times, Dare to be!

Be Thankful

Author Unknown

Be thankful that you don't already have everything you desire.
If you did, what would there be to look forward to?
Be thankful when you don't know something,
for it gives you the opportunity to learn.

Be thankful for the difficult times.
During those times you grow.
Be thankful for your limitations,
because they give you opportunities for improvement.
Be thankful for each new challenge,
because it will build your strength and character.

Be thankful for your mistakes.
They will teach you valuable lessons.
Be thankful when you're tired and weary,
because it means you've made a difference.

It's easy to be thankful for the good things.
A life of rich fulfillment comes to those who
are also thankful for the setbacks.
Gratitude can turn a negative into a positive.
Find a way to be thankful for your troubles,
and they can become your blessings.

Believe

By Wish Belkin

Believe in rewards that await you,
believe in the harvest in store.

Believe that the spring will awaken,
believe you'll be sowing once more.

Believe that there's a tomorrow,
where no one cares if you can't dance.

Believe in the future's promise,
each new day brings a new chance.

Believe you can make you goals happen,
they're just dreams with a deadline attached.

Believe that you have the power,
believe that you're more than a match.

Believe in a shared existence,
you're not alone this is true.

Believe that right now there is someone,
who believes in the wonder that's you.

The Power of Words

Author Unknown

A group of frogs were traveling through the woods, and two of them fell into a deep pit. All the other frogs gathered around the pit. When they saw how deep the pit was, they told the two frogs that they were as good as dead.

The two frogs ignored the comments and tried to jump up out of the pit with all of their might. The other frogs kept telling them to stop, that they were as good as dead. Finally, one of the frogs took heed to what the other frogs were saying and gave up. He fell down and died.

The other frog continued to jump as hard as he could. Once again, the crowd of frogs yelled at him to stop the pain and just die. He jumped even harder and finally made it out.

When he got out, the other frogs said, "Did you not hear us?" The frog explained to them that he was deaf. He thought they were encouraging him the entire time.

Last thoughts

Once again I would like to thank all the authors who shared these inspirational messages with us. I would also like to thank the people who email, post on their web site and take the time to share these messages with others.

I must remind you of my most valued words once again; **knowledge + action = results**. Even if these quotes empower you or touch you in a special way, they are useless if you do not use them as fuel to take action. Dale Carnegie and Benjamin Franklin are just two of a countless number of successful people throughout time who had the same core attributes that equaled success and fulfillment. Remember the old saying, "if it isn't broke don't try to fix it". If you take the time to create a core of success inside of you, then fulfillment in all areas of your life is inevitable. There is no reason you can't leave your mark and live each day with passion.

A few last minute things to ponder

◆ What you believe you can do is what you will do. Believe big!

◆ No one has ever succeeded in life without experiencing failure or obstacles.

◆ Turn your obstacles in to your motivation.

◆ You are not alone.

◆ Embrace change, without it things will stay the same.

◆ Focus on solutions always.

◆ Avoid wasting energy on things you can't change.

◆ There is nothing in life anyone else has that you can't have.

◆ Empowering relationships are a keystone to success.

- Treat others as you wish to be treated.

- Take advice and comments only from those who inspire you.

- No one can make you feel inferior without your permission.

- You are the captain of your ship.

- Be a doer in life not talker.

- Your past does not determine your future.

- Find the true purpose of your goals and they shall become a reality.

And for those of you wanting to make more money or start you own business:

- There are millions of millionaires that started with nothing.

- It does not take money to make money.

- Surround yourself with people who have more than you.

- Adversity is the mother of invention.

- Your income potential is not determined solely by your education or your blood line.

- Knowledge plus action equals results.

- Don't over analyze and ponder—take action or move on.

I hope this added section of inspiration affected you like it did for me while I was putting it all together. In fact I am going to take this last section "Inspiration is Timeless" and put it on the www.totallyfulfilled.com web site. Just click on the free bonus section and you will be able to view and download this entire chapter. Then you can print out the quotes, stories or poems that affect or inspire you the most.

I have dedicated the next nine pages for worksheets, reference guides and reminders to help you stay on track and focused on your way to a totally fulfilled life. Remember passive people tend to have poor results. So roll your sleeves up, grab a pen and dig in. Your future awaits you.

Beliefs Worksheet

Limiting Beliefs

_____

_____

_____

_____

_____

_____

_____

_____

_____

_____

_____

_____

_____

_____

_____

_____

Limitless Beliefs

_____

_____

_____

_____

_____

_____

_____

_____

_____

_____

_____

_____

_____

_____

_____

_____

What Drives You?

_____

_____

_____

_____

_____

_____

_____

_____

_____

_____

_____

_____

_____

_____

_____

_____

_____

Comparison Chart

Present Reality	Totally Fulfilled Life
_____	_____
_____	_____
_____	_____
_____	_____
_____	_____
_____	_____
_____	_____
_____	_____
_____	_____
_____	_____
_____	_____
_____	_____
_____	_____
_____	_____
_____	_____
_____	_____

Master Goal Sheet

_____   _____

_____   _____

_____   _____

_____   _____

_____   _____

_____   _____

_____   _____

_____   _____

_____   _____

_____   _____

_____   _____

_____   _____

_____   _____

_____   _____

_____   _____

Master Goal Sheet

Category I
Goal:_____

    Reason:_____

    _____

    _____

    Feeling:_____

    _____

Goal:_____

    Reason:_____

    _____

    _____

    Feeling:_____

    _____

Goal:_____

    Reason:_____

    _____

    _____

    Feeling:_____

    _____

Master Goal Sheet

Category II

Goal:_____

     Reason:_____

     _____

     _____

     Feeling:_____

     _____

Goal:_____

     Reason:_____

     _____

     _____

     Feeling:_____

     _____

Goal:_____

     Reason:_____

     _____

     _____

     Feeling:_____

     _____

Master Goal Sheet

Category III

Goal:_____

    Reason:_____

    _____

    _____

    Feeling:_____

    _____

Goal:_____

    Reason:_____

    _____

    _____

    Feeling:_____

    _____

Goal:_____

    Reason:_____

    _____

    _____

    Feeling:_____

    _____

Fun Goal Sheet

Goal:_____   Goal:_____

    Reason:_____   Reason:_____

    _____   _____

    Feeling:_____   Feeling:_____

    _____   _____

Goal:_____   Goal:_____

    Reason:_____   Reason:_____

    _____   _____

    Feeling:_____   Feeling:_____

    _____   _____

Goal:_____   Goal:_____

    Reason:_____   Reason:_____

    _____   _____

    Feeling:_____   Feeling:_____

    _____   _____

Goal:_____   Goal:_____

    Reason:_____   Reason:_____

    _____   _____

    Feeling:_____   Feeling:_____

    _____   _____

On Track for a Great Day

- Wake up, jump out of bed as if you were going to pick up a million dollars.

- Look in the mirror and erase the stress from the previous day.

- Put your shoulders back, open your eyes wide, and take a deep breath.

- Take a minute to search why you are grateful:

_____

_____

_____

- Give thanks to the special people in your life and the ones who have touched you along the way:

_____

_____

_____

- Be proud of yourself and reflect on the accomplishments you have achieved:

_____

_____

_____

- Wish good things for those who may have tough obstacles.

- Think of the things you would love to accomplish that day:

_____

_____

_____

A Final Message From Dean

Nothing would be more rewarding for me than knowing that you are living your best life possible. You now have everything you need to live a life of wealth, health, love, prosperity, and abundance.

But before we part ways, please know that I am committed to your long-term success and fulfillment. And to further prove my dedication, please go to *www.totallyfulfilled.com* and receive additional tools and a special motivational audio from me. It's all free. Plus, you can learn about our mentor program and our financial education products.

Remember, the most important investment you have in life is *you*.

About the Author

Dean Graziosi was born in Marlboro, New York, a small farm town about 70 miles north of New York City. Dean's challenging childhood left him with a desire to find success on many levels.

Growing up in a financially troubled and broken home, Dean decided at a very young age to follow his entrepreneurial spirit and go for more out of life than what he saw around him. Starting with just a high school education and no money, Dean has been able to generate tens of millions of dollars in his life, using a variety of teachable techniques.

Dean is known nationally for "keeping it simple." His unique approach to life allowed him to start successful businesses and relationships as early as high school. Dean went on to own and run several profitable companies in his hometown.

In 1998, he decided he wanted to share his strategies for success with the country. He authored *Motor Millions*, a step-by-step course to build wealth with automobiles. Then he went on to author *Think A Little Different*, a guide to building a real estate fortune.

He has been on national TV since 1999, helping regular people achieve tremendous financial success. His audios, videos, and books have sold over a million copies to date.

Along his journey, he developed what he calls a "core" for success that, once applied, can allow anyone to reach Total Fulfillment and success in *all* areas of life not just financial.

Dean is often heard to say, "I have been living life in fast-forward, and the incredible experiences in my life have taught me not only what to do to reach Total Fulfillment but also what *not* to do."

His passion and ultimate goal is for this book—and the ones to follow—to let people know that they can absolutely replace stress, fear, scarcity, pain, low self-esteem, frustration, lack of fulfillment, and unhappiness with success, financial independence, love, courage, confidence, peace, happiness, faith, and Total Fulfillment in all areas of life.